CONTENTS

THE NURSERY TEACHER IN ACTION

Margaret Lally is a freelance early years consultant and has contributed to in-service courses for nursery and infant staff in many parts of the UK. She trained as an early years teacher, and has taught in infant as well as nursery classes. However, she is a specialist in nursery education. Her experience has included educational home visiting; lecturing on an NNEB course; work as an early years co-ordinator in two ILEA divisions; headship of a new nursery school in inner London; and work as a development officer at the National Children's Bureau Under Fives Unit. She has written articles for journals; two papers in the NCB Highlight series, ·*Four Year Olds in School* (1989, No. 88) and *Curriculum for Three to Five Year Olds* (1989, No. 89); a course report, *An Integrated Approach to the National Curriculum in the Early Years 3–7* (NCB, 1989); and is co-editor of *Working With Children: Developing a Curriculum for the Early Years* (NCB/Nottingham Educational Supplies, 1989). She is an active member of the Early Years Curriculum Group and was one of the authors of *Early Childhood Education: The Early Years Curriculum and the National Curriculum* (Trentham Books, 1989).

THE NURSERY TEACHER IN ACTION

MARGARET LALLY

P·C·P
Paul Chapman
Publishing Ltd

The term 'nurse' used throughout this book refers, naturally, to 'nursery nurse' and has been used to avoid repetition.

First published 1991
Paul Chapman Publishing Ltd
144 Liverpool Road
London
N1 1LA

British Library Cataloguing in Publication Data
Lally, Margaret
   The nursery teacher in action.
   1. Nursery schools. Teaching
   I. Title
   372.1102

   ISBN 1–85396–131–0

Typeset by Inforum Typesetting, Portsmouth
Printed and bound by Athenæum Press Ltd.,
Gateshead, Tyne & Wear.

INTRODUCTION

According to the Education, Science and Arts Committee (ESAC) (1989, p. xlv) 'There is a need for DES and LEAs to examine ways of giving stronger emphasis to the value and status of nursery teachers.'

The aim of this book is to help DES and LEAs – and headteachers, teachers, governors and the general public – to do exactly that. It has been written in celebration of the skilled nursery teacher. In offering a detailed discussion of her responsibilities and achievements, the book sets out to dispel the myth that 'anyone can work with the little ones'. Yes they can – badly! This book is about early education of the highest quality. This education is to be found in nursery schools and classes staffed by qualified nursery teachers and nursery nurses.

Anyone who has ever worked as a nursery teacher will understand the difficulties and dilemmas involved in this role. In spite of their four-year training (at the same level as all other teachers), they are often regarded by the general public and even by their colleagues as little more than baby minders. There are many possible reasons for this. Nursery education is not really any nearer to becoming part of statutory education provision than it was at the time of the 1972 White Paper (DES, 1972) which proposed that within ten years all 3- and 4-year-olds whose parents wished it would have a nursery education place. Nearly twenty years later less than a quarter of this age group have a place in a nursery class or school (ESAC, 1989).

This shortage of places has meant that many parents, politicians and teachers have not experienced nursery education, and have no concept of the role of the nursery teacher and of the qualified nursery nurse. Their experience of provision for 3- to 5-year-olds may be confined to voluntary playgroups, private nurseries or to the reception classes, which over 60 per cent of 4-year-olds now attend. None of these are nursery education as defined by DES guidelines (DES, 1972).

The shortage of statutory provision for young children has led to a reliance on the voluntary and private sector. Indeed, this reliance has been encouraged by the government who, in its response to the ESAC report, asserted its belief that 'there is scope for substantial private and voluntary sector involvement in this field' and went on to add that it would 'seek ways of maximising the contribution which such provision can make to the fulfilment of demand for high quality nursery education' (DES, 1989b). It is not surprising that there is confusion about the nature of nursery education when politicians use the phrase so loosely, and refuse to admit publicly that what a lot of young children are being offered is a cheap substitute which bears no comparison with the real thing. Many parents have seen through the deception, however, and are making their views clear – a majority want their children to attend a nursery school or class (Bone, 1977; ESAC, 1988, p. 189). The Association of Metropolitan Authorities believe this preference is due to the parents' growing understanding of the educational experience offered by nursery education (ESAC, 1988).

At a time when the spotlight is on services for young children, it has never been more important to be clear about what is currently being offered, and yet this clarity often seems to be missing from discussions. It seems sometimes as though the quality of different types of provision and of the training of the staff involved are secondary concerns.

Often the emphasis seems to be on increasing the quantity of nursery places as cheaply as possible. Alongside the increase in private and workplace provision, nursery education appears to be under threat yet again. Anecdotal evidence reveals that some nursery teachers have been redeployed into primary classes to cover staff shortages – the nursery class being closed at least temporarily. Community charge capping has forced some LEAs to prune their already tight budgets, and as usual all non-statutory provision is at risk. LEAs deserve some sympathy, however, since none of us would enjoy having to prioritize services as they have to.

Compounding these difficulties is the shortage of early years trained teachers (ESAC, 1989) which is likely to continue (David, 1990). Consequently, many nursery age children are already being taught by teachers (in nursery and reception classes) who have not been trained to teach them. It is clear from talking to some of these teachers that they are totally unaware of their responsibilities in relation to this age group. Some express frustration because the children do not respond as expected, while others show an alarming lack of sensitivity to emotional needs. This is not their fault, since no one can be expected to understand what a job involves unless they have been trained to do it. However, while an untrained computer operator will at worst damage a machine, the inadequately trained early years teacher is placed in a position where she could harm the child's development.

To the credit of many of these teachers, they quickly realize their inadequacies and seek out training courses at the earliest opportunity. However, it is debatable whether a short in-service course could meet their needs. It is certainly no substitute for the kind of child development-based initial training nursery teachers have traditionally received. Unfortunately, some teachers placed in this position blame their own inadequacies on the children – they must have extreme behaviour problems, or 'poor homes', or some other difficulty. These children are labelled before they reach statutory school age.

We have a wealth of evidence (referred to in the book) which demonstrates how teachers can educate this age group badly, and which also makes clear what 3- and 4-year-olds need. This evidence has highlighted the need for well-qualified staff, who fully recognize their responsibility to children and their families. It is difficult to understand why this evidence has not resulted in a massive increase in nursery education – it is impossible to understand how anyone could think that minimally trained volunteers could offer this high-quality education.

The knowledge and skills of the nursery teacher are still misunderstood. To the casual observer she must look like any other adult working with young children. Even her nursery nurse colleagues do not always appreciate the breadth and depth of her concerns – except perhaps when they have trained to be a teacher themselves. Perhaps it takes one to recognize one! A nursery nurse who had just completed her teacher training after years of nursery nursing commented 'I never realized there was so much involved in teaching.'

This book focuses on the skills, knowledge and attitudes which are at the heart of effective nursery teaching. The nursery teacher is referred to as 'she' in recognition of the fact that it is still a predominantly female profession, and to acknowledge that women must be given most of the credit for achievements in the field. I believe the growing number of similarly skilled men now involved in the profession would want the women who supported them in the early stages of their career to be given this recognition. In no way does the use of 'she' imply that nursery teaching is, or can only be, a female profession. Where possible, I have used the words of experienced nursery teachers (including men) collected on in-service courses in many parts of Britain, and all the practice referred to reflects developments taking place in the nursery classroom, and is not based on an impractical ideal. Having made that clear, it is important to stress that this is a book about the most innovative nursery teachers – those who have developed, and are continuing to develop, their practice in response to new evidence. They will recognize themselves and I am grateful to them all for the inspiration they have given me.

Those who do not recognize themselves and their practice must ask themselves why. It is certainly not the intention to imply that any of the practices referred to are the only way of approaching an issue. However, although no prescription for practice is offered – the most meaningful practice is always developed by individual teams – the issues and concerns outlined in the book are all ones which every nursery teacher must address in her own work. The practical suggestions in the book highlight just some of the ways effective nursery teachers are translating principles into practice.

There is widespread agreement that nursery teaching involves:

- leadership responsibilities;
- understanding the developmental needs of young children and the role of families in that development;
- recordkeeping;
- enabling all children to reach their full potential through a curriculum based on individual needs;
- evaluation – of the provision made, of the children's experience, and of oneself.

These are complex responsibilities. They are not easy to describe or carry out, but it is currently vital that they are better understood and articulated both within and outside of the profession. This book makes a contribution to this understanding.

Although it is intended primarily for use by those involved in teaching 3- to 5-year-olds and by those planning (or training) to work with this age group, this book should also be of interest to everyone else concerned with the education of young children. Parents, governors and national and local policy-makers would all benefit from heightening their awareness of the professional skills involved in nursery teaching. Maybe they will be inspired to join the growing movement to enable all children to benefit from these skills.

This book should also be of interest to other under-5s' workers, in particular the nursery nurses who work so effectively alongside nursery teachers. I chose to focus on the nursery teacher, but I hope that NNEB trained staff will not feel that their skills are unacknowledged. Nursery education gains its strength and quality from the *two* professionals involved. An effective nursery teacher plus an effective nursery nurse equals a very powerful combination of expertise. Nursery nurses were involved in developing all the initiatives described in this book – many of these initiatives would not have been possible without the benefit of their complementary skills. However, teachers carry ultimate responsibility for what happens in a nursery class. It was the intention in this book to focus narrowly on these responsibilities, and to provide a positive view of the teacher as a team leader, who regards the nursery nurse as a highly valued colleague.

This has been a difficult book to write. Effective nursery teachers make their work look easy. When talking to them, many of them modestly play down their expertise – they are quite rightly aware that there is much which could be done better, and are reluctant to accept that they are already doing the job well. Much of what they do they appear to do intuitively, but considerably more than intuition is required to enable them to operate on a range of different levels with children and adults, adapting their knowledge and skills and varying their approach in response to the individuals they are interacting with. They are only able to work in this way because of their training and because of their willingness to reflect upon their experiences, and to evaluate and revise their practice.

It is difficult, and it seems artificial, to separate the many strands involved in the nursery teacher's work since they all overlap and link with each other, and yet unless we do try to separate them, it is not possible to understand fully the complexity of the work. Any attempt at separation is bound to be inadequate in some ways. It is my hope, however, that this book will make a strong contribution to the debate on quality education for young children, and that it will persuade parents and policy-makers that nursery teachers must be involved. It should also remind the teachers themselves that they still need to convince others of the value of their expertise.

The 'points for discussion' at the end of each chapter are intended to support nursery teachers as they evaluate their work either alone, with their team, or on training courses. They may also help visitors to nursery classes to understand what they are seeing.

The emphasis throughout is on the key issues involved in nursery teaching and the reasons why these cannot be ignored. What is involved in these issues is explored and some examples of how they are being tackled in practice are given. The overall impression should be one of nursery teaching as a dynamic occupation, involving teachers in an ongoing investigation of themselves and of the needs of the children and families they work with. It is a book describing the current state of the art, but always (and particularly the final chapter) with a view to future concerns and developments.

In order to avoid repetition, the nursery teacher and nursery nurse are sometimes referred to as the teacher and the nurse.

ACKNOWLEDGEMENTS

It was no easy task to persuade me that I could write this book or to keep me going once I had started! I would therefore like to thank:

Vicky Hurst whose enthusiasm for nursery education, and for my work has been totally infectious. In particular, her ability to turn panic into laughter has been much appreciated.

Wendy Scott for her belief in my ability, and for her continuing support and encouragement.

Ann Robinson for help with the references.

Richard Lally for his consistent patience throughout the highs and lows, and for his help with wordprocessing, editing and indexing.

The staff, children and parents of all the schools I have worked in for their inspiration.

The many nursery teachers and advisers I have met in the course of my in-service work for their willingness to share ideas and concerns, and for inspiring me to tackle the difficult issues with them.

Last but not least, my love and thanks to Irmgard and Ewart Edgington for giving me the kind of start in life which enabled me to believe I could achieve something (in spite of what some teachers told me!).

This book is dedicated to them all.

1

LEADING THE NURSERY TEAM

If you ask any newly qualified nursery teacher about which aspect of her job she is most apprehensive, it is almost certain that she will reply 'leading a team' or words to that effect. If she does not give this answer, it is equally certain that her training has not prepared her adequately for the complexity of her future role as a manager of other adults. No other teacher is expected to take on this role, which often involves leading older more experienced adults, from the very first day of her career.

Support for Leadership

The support offered to teachers to help them tackle this role will vary, and depends to a large extent on whether they work in a nursery class attached to a primary school or in a separate nursery school, and on the ability of tutors and colleagues to understand the challenges involved in managing adults as well as children. This understanding may only come from actual experience of nursery teaching, and given the shortage of teacher trainers and primary teachers with this experience, it is not surprising that many nursery teachers feel they are left to cope as well as they can!

It is ironic that nursery teachers receive so little help with what is undoubtedly the most important aspect of their job. Everything they do is affected directly or indirectly by their approach to the leadership role. It does not take them long to realize this, and to start making requests for in-service courses on interpersonal and management skills. These requests are not always taken as seriously as they should be, and with the continued lack of resources for early years training generally, it is difficult to see the situation improving. Within this climate, increasing numbers of nursery teachers are setting up local, self-help groups and are gaining support and encouragement from sharing issues and concerns with others of like mind. It is not surprising that informally organized discussions of this kind regularly focus on aspects of the leadership role – in particular the challenges involved. In this chapter, we explore these challenges and some strategies for coping with them. But what is meant by the nursery team, and what are the tasks involved in leading it?

Who Makes Up the Nursery Team?

The simple answer to this question is: everyone who comes into contact with the children during the school day! However, it is worth identifying who these people might be in the interests of demonstrating the daunting nature of the leadership task.

The Basic Team

As an absolute minimum, the nursery class team will consist of the nursery teacher and the NNEB (or increasingly BTEC) trained nursery nurse – the basic team recommended by the DES to work with a group of twenty-five or twenty-six 3- to 5-year-old children. In larger units, one (usually experienced) nursery teacher may be expected to lead a team consisting of up to two other teachers and up to four nursery nurses.

Nursery nurses complete a two-year training course at a college of further education. This is primarily a practical training in all aspects of the care and education of children from birth to 7 years of age. Nursery teachers, on the other hand, complete an academically rigorous training in the theory and practice of the education of 3- to 8- or 9-year-olds – the same kind of course as those training to teach older children. These two types of training are complementary and, when both team members understand the contribution they can make jointly to the children's total experience, the result is the highest possible quality of care and education for 3- to 5-year-old children.

It is essential that nursery teachers know what is involved in nursery nurse training so that they can encourage full use of their colleagues' skills.

Other Staff in the Team

In addition to this basic team, nursery schools and classes where full-time places are offered will also employ supervisors to work with the children during the lunch-time period. Meal times are considered to offer tremendous potential for conversation with, and learning for, young children, so the role of these supervisors is a crucial one, and guidance and support have to be offered to these usually untrained staff.

Schools and classes which admit children with special educational needs may also employ staff to support individual children in order that they can continue to attend mainstream provision, once a statement of needs has been produced. Similarly, schools with a high proportion of bilingual children often employ staff to offer home language support.

These support staff may be part time or full time, and can be trained or untrained depending on the needs of the children they are supporting. In either case, they will work as a part of the nursery team and need to be included in the nursery teacher's management responsibilities.

It is important to emphasize that support and guidance also need to be offered to relief staff who replace absent nursery nurses, meal supervisors and support staff.

Although not a regular part of the nursery team, there are a number of other members of school staff who regularly come into contact with the children and therefore have an influence on them. These staff may include the school secretary, the caretaker, and other teachers (including the headteacher). Although the nursery teacher is not directly responsible for managing these staff, she is responsible in her role as leader of the nursery team for ensuring that they are all aware of, and act consistently with, her aims for the children's learning.

Additions to the Team

The basic staffing ratio of one teacher and one nursery nurse working with up to twenty-six children is not a particularly generous one. Most nursery education establishments therefore offer opportunities for a range of other adults to involve themselves in work with the children. These other adults include students (on a whole range of secondary school and college courses including teaching, nursery nursing, and other community work courses), parents, members of the local community, and other professionals such as the school nurse, speech therapist, and health visitor. The contribution of all of these adults enriches the children's experience, but at the same time makes additional demands on the nursery teacher, who has to ensure that they understand the ethos of the nursery, and the nature of their involvement, as well as offering them the support they need to become involved. Many nursery teachers have discovered that the addition of an immature fifth former, who overexcites the children, is more of a hindrance than a help!

Parents as Team Members

It is worth looking in more detail at the role of parents as members of the nursery team. Nursery teachers and nursery nurses provide children with their first experience of the education system and are expected to make the transition from home to school a positive one. This requires them to work closely with parents (before and during the child's attendance at nursery) in the interests of continuity of experience for the children (Blatchford, Battle and Mays, 1982). It is in everyone's interest to ensure that all parents feel they are a part of the school team and can continue the contribution they have already made to the education of their children. Indeed, many primary headteachers acknowledge the vital work the nursery staff undertake to encourage the parents' confidence in, and commitment to, the school.

Acknowledgement does not necessarily mean that the skills or time involved in this undertaking are fully recognized and nursery staff have not always been able to articulate the liaison work they do so skilfully. How many teachers of older children regularly fit home visiting, daily informal chats and sharing of concerns, discussions of children's progress, and support of parents working in the class into their daily routine, alongside all the curriculum development work – without any additional time or resources? Nursery teachers communicate and work with parents in these ways because they know that they cannot provide a high quality education for the children unless they do. Just as infant teachers need to make themselves aware of, and build on, the children's nursery experience, so nursery teachers must familiarize themselves with and develop the experiences each child has gained at home and in the community.

Aspects of Leadership

Being a leader makes many different demands on the nursery teacher, depending on the other adults she is involving in her work – these demands are in addition to the demands made on her by the children, who also require her to adopt a range of different roles which will be explored later.

It is also clear that being a leader does not just involve telling people what to do or leading from the front. Leading for the nursery teacher can also involve befriending, explaining, supporting, respecting, valuing, enabling, partnering, listening, including, co-ordinating, co-operating and sharing. No wonder the role seems so daunting!

Nursery Leaders – Born or Made?

The amount of support currently offered to nursery teachers to help them take on the leadership role seems to indicate either that the skills involved are not recognized, or that leadership is believed to be an intuitive process. It is obvious from talking to groups of nursery teachers that they would welcome and benefit from specific training to help them with this part of their work. Many of the problems they face in their daily work can be traced to difficulties with the leadership role. Some of these difficulties are examined later in this chapter. Usually, they are caused by nursery teachers not being clear about the purposes of the leadership role. In other words, they are not clear about what they and their team are trying to do.

The Industrial Society (1969, p. 3) points out that managers need to understand what actions they need to take in order to be effective, and provides a useful 'working model for the leader'. This model emphasizes three areas of functioning for a team leader: 'achieving the task', 'building the team' and 'developing individuals'. These three areas act on each other, with effective leaders needing to pay attention to all three areas, often simultaneously. This is offered primarily as a model of industrial or business leadership but, when translated into the language of education, is also relevant for the nursery teacher struggling to understand her responsibilities.

Although the three areas are considered separately below from the point of view of the team leader (i.e. the nursery teacher), it is important to stress that in reality they overlap and that responsibility for ensuring they are covered is often shared between members of the team. This will be clarified through the examples that are given.

Achieving the Task

Before the team leader or the team can think about achieving anything, it is necessary for them to define the tasks which they need to accomplish.

Clarifying principles

The nursery teacher has overall responsibility for ensuring that the children in her class are offered an education appropriate to their needs, and consistent with current thinking in relation to the theory and practice of early childhood education. This responsibility requires her (with the help of local authority guidelines, in-service courses, and reading) to make herself aware of current developments, and to clarify the principles on which she will base her work.

Only if she understands these principles will she be able to identify ways of translating them into practice. For example, research into the contribution of parents to early childhood education has demonstrated how important it is for nursery staff to work closely with parents so that they can understand and build on the experiences children have gained before starting school (Tizard and Hughes, 1984; Wells, 1986). An awareness and understanding of this research leads to the formation of a principle, i.e. that parents have an important complementary role to play in their child's education, and to a commitment to developing that principle in practice, e.g. involving parents in recordkeeping by providing them with opportunities to share their knowledge of their child in the home situation.

Teachers whose work is not underpinned by principles which they can back up with research evidence, are less likely to be able to see a clear direction for the development of their practice, and more likely to fall victim to the many pressures which currently exist, e.g. the pressure to teach in inappropriate, formal ways. They are also less likely to be able to provide a strong lead for the other adults they work with. These other adults may not have had opportunities to learn about current developments in early childhood education, and may need sensitive support from the nursery teacher to enable them to develop their understanding of the issues at their own pace.

It is the nursery teacher's responsibility to set the overall standard for her class, and to ensure that her team understand what is involved and the reasons why they need to develop their work in a particular way. This process is one of defining the ground rules and reaching some shared understandings. It is explored further in the section on team building (below).

Defining the tasks

The nursery team's tasks incorporate all aspects of nursery education such as the organization of the learning environment and the daily routine; admissions procedures; the development of curriculum policy and practice statements and of planning and recordkeeping systems; the promotion of equal opportunities policies and practices; the involvement of parents and the wider community; and the development of links with the infant classes. It is up to the nursery teacher to ensure that team members understand what the tasks are and that they are tackled, since she is ultimately responsible and accountable for what does or does not happen in her class.

The details of these tasks will have been clarified at least partly by whole school development plans and local authority policy statements and guidelines. For example, a particular school may have decided to attempt to develop a whole school approach to planning the curriculum. In this situation, the nursery teacher would be expected to work out, in consultation with her team and with her specialist knowledge of the needs of young children in mind, exactly what is involved in planning the curriculum for under-5s and how this task is to be approached in her class. This involves deciding, within the framework of the team's own principles and any external guidelines available to them, an appropriate, meaningful and manageable method for them. In the context of whole school policy-making, the nursery teacher is responsible for representing her team's approach to planning the curriculum for the nursery class to the rest of the staff, governors, parents and so on.

Principles are important for the teacher and her team. If, for example, they believe that 'what children can do, not what they cannot do, is the starting point in children's learning' (EYCG, 1989, p. 3), they will want to ensure that their planning builds on children's existing interests and experiences, and is flexible enough to enable adults to develop a responsive rather than a directive curriculum. They will strongly resist the pressure which some nursery staff are facing to produce neat plans for a year or more's work. They will see planning in terms of possibilities for learning, and not in terms of certainty. Above all they will be able to argue their case effectively.

It is essential that those who understand the needs of young children are given responsibility for defining what is involved in curriculum development. Many teachers have welcomed the opportunities they have been given in recent years to inform, or even to lead, whole school policy-making. Their approaches to curriculum development have provided a firm foundation on which other teachers can build.

Breaking down the tasks

Defining the nursery team's tasks, deciding which one to tackle first, beginning to identify what is involved in achieving it, and ensuring that it is achieved in practice, require the teacher to prioritize.

Some teachers on in-service courses complain that they cannot be effective leaders because 'they have too much to do' and because 'there is no time'! It is true that the day-to-day demands of a busy nursery class can seem totally overwhelming at times, and can lead to a crisis management approach where things are dealt with as they arise. There are times when this approach is unavoidable, since some things need to be dealt with there and then, but generally time is more effectively utilized and outcomes more satisfactory if task priorities are set (identifying the task, or part of the task, to be worked on first) and plans made for action (identifying what needs to be done, deciding who will do what, what they will need and by when they aim to have completed it).

When priorities are set in this way it is important that what has been planned is achievable. Nursery teachers have to make difficult decisions about what it is realistic to expect of themselves and others, in the time and with the resources available. Many have learnt the hard way that it is better to start slowly and on a small scale and achieve something, than to have big ideas which end up being abandoned due to sheer frustration with the enormity of the task. If, for example, it has been decided that at least some curriculum planning should relate to the staff's observations of the children's interests and achievements, it is better for each member of staff to concentrate on observing one child or a small group of children, and to have something to work from, than to try to observe the whole class and end up observing no one because the task seemed so enormous it was impossible to get started!

Prioritizing is possibly the most difficult part of the nursery teacher's job. All teachers complain that their job is unmanageable and that too much is expected of them. Nursery teachers are no exception.

At times when the pressure to improve or develop ten aspects of practice at once seems totally overwhelming, it is not surprising that prioritizing seems impossible. After all how can you concentrate on developing provision for outdoor play when your recordkeeping system needs improving, you need a written policy statement to explain your approach to reading, and the local authority adviser has just told you you need to change the way you plan the curriculum!

This is why, when a group of experienced nursery teachers on an inservice course are asked 'which aspects of your current practice would you most like to develop?' they answer 'everything!' By saying this they are acknowledging their awareness of the need to regularly review everything they do, and the impossibility of ever doing any part of their job to their complete satisfaction. This is a problem only if they allow their awareness to overwhelm them and prevent them from tacklng anything at all.

If attention is not focused primarily on one thing at a time, nothing receives the consideration it requires and very little is achieved. It is the teacher's job to ensure that achievements to date are acknowledged (i.e. those aspects of practice which have already been developed), and to identify the next step (i.e. the area which most needs development and which the staff team are capable of tackling), while keeping in mind longer-term plans (i.e. those things which need to be worked on in the future). Knowing where you have come from, where you are now, where you are going next, and where you hope to be in the future is the best way to reassure yourself and your team that progress is being made; and to protect yourself from the pressures. Wise headteachers and early years inspectors/advisers respect and support nursery teachers who approach their work in this way.

Involving the team in prioritizing

Although the nursery teacher is responsible for prioritizing, this does not mean she should do this alone. As well as taking into account external influences (in the form of the whole school development plan and any local authority and national priorities), the skilled teacher knows that greater co-operation will be achieved if all members of the basic team are involved in deciding what to tackle first.

There are many ways of approaching this. In a small team of two or three, where basic trust has been established, a discussion is probably the best way forward.

One teacher asked the nursery nurse she worked with to think about the aspects of nursery life she was pleased with and thought worked well, and which she was not pleased with and did not work well. Both members of the basic team thought about this for a week and made a few notes to bring to a discussion. They then shared their ideas and discovered that the aspect of their provision they were both least pleased with was the lunchtime period. Together they were able to identify what was going wrong, what they would like to achieve for the children and themselves (their aims), and what steps they could take to achieve their aims in practice. The main points from the discussion were recorded by the teacher for future reference. Since organization of lunchtimes involved the meals supervisor, the nursery teacher followed up this meeting of the basic team with a discussion with her, explaining what had happened and asking for her views. In this situation the nursery teacher acted as co-ordinator – making sure that all members of the team were involved and had a chance to have a say even if they could not be present at all meetings. The outcome of these discussions was a set of policy and practice guidelines to inform staff supervising mealtimes. All staff involved were committed to them because their contribution had been valued and included. The guidelines were shared with the rest of the school staff and with parents of full-time children, so that everyone could gain an insight into what the nursery staff were trying to achieve. They were also shown to, and discussed with, all students and relief staff who came to work in the class.

In a larger team, where some staff may lack the confidence to express their views openly, e.g. in a large nursery school, a structured questionnaire, filled in anonymously, can be a helpful approach to prioritizing.

Dowling (1988) includes a sample questionnaire adapted from the Schools Council document *Guidelines for Internal Review and Development in Schools* (1984). Some nursery teachers offer parents the chance to be involved in filling in a similar questionnaire about the strengths and weaknesses of the education their children are being offered.

Prioritizing democratically in this way can produce unexpected results – the area of practice a majority of the team identifies as being most in need of development, may not be the area which the team leader would have selected. In this situation it is important that the nursery teacher remembers the other parts of her leadership role – in particular her team-building responsibilities.

Team Building

In order to identify and achieve the tasks involved in nursery education the whole team must be involved and committed. Many a new nursery teacher has come to grief because she has plunged enthusiastically into the task as she saw it, and antagonized the other members of her team in the process.

So what does team building involve? Primarily it requires the nursery teacher to help all members of staff to understand that they need to work as a team – that is that they need to reach some shared understandings on which they will base their work. This seems obvious and yet discussions with nursery staff reveal that this fundamental need is sometimes neglected, leading to situations where individuals function quite separately from each other.

Nursery teachers have to understand that they are not self-sufficient, and depend on the support of their team for the successful running of their class. A basic leadership function is therefore to ensure regular opportunities for team discussion, both formal and informal. These discussions have a triple function. They provide the teacher with insights into the attitudes and understanding of team members – in particular they enable her to identify the stage of development her team has reached. They also offer all team members the chance to put forward their point of view and share in the decision-making process, and finally they reinforce the idea of a shared team approach. It is difficult to see how any sense of collective purpose could be achieved without these regular discussions.

Co-ordination and communication

It is not always possible for all members of the team to meet at the same time, and the nursery teacher has to act as co-ordinator and communicator of discussions. It is through this co-ordination and communication that the teacher constantly reinforces the idea of a collective team approach. She acts as a link between team members, and also between the team and the outside world – parents, colleagues, governors, the local authority and any national developments.

In order to co-ordinate and communicate effectively, the nursery teacher must realize that no two teams are the same and that each team will have 'its own personality, its own power, its own attitudes, its own standards and its own needs' (The Industrial Society, 1969, p. 10). She has to find out about and respond to the particular characteristics of the people she works with. This sometimes means putting her own needs and interests to one side and concentrating on the needs and interests of others. There will be times when she will want to shield the team from outside pressures she knows they are not yet ready to deal with, and there will also be times when she will want to encourage the team to share their achievements with others. At all times she will want to emphasize the unity of the team particularly in terms of practice.

Teams are made up of individuals with different points of view and unity comes from working together to reach a shared understanding of the principles and tasks mentioned previously. Having involved the team in clarifying principles and prioritizing tasks it is up to the nursery teacher to check that everyone is committed to translating these into practice.

From time to time this will involve her in asking why particular members of the team are not working consistently with team objectives. Is it because they were not fully involved in, or did not understand, the discussion? Or because they disagreed but were afraid or unwilling to say so? Or because they have been unable to translate policy into their own practice? Or some other reason? The answer to these questions will provide the teacher with clues for evaluating her leadership skills.

At this point she realizes that relating to the team as a group can only work if she also relates to each member of the team as an individual, since it only takes one individual to sabotage (intentionally or unintentionally) the work of the rest of the team. For example, a team's work on encouraging children to be less dependent on adults was hampered by a member of staff who persisted in doing things for the children which they could easily have done for themselves, such as putting on the plastic apron for water play. The children soon learnt which adult to go to if they wanted to save themselves some effort and other adults in the team became resentful because their colleague seemed to be taking the easy way out – it is often easier and less time consuming, at least in the short term, to do things for young children than to encourage them to try to do it for themselves.

Clearly it is the nursery teacher's responsibility to help this individual to understand how she is undermining the work of the whole team.

Developing Individuals

While most people enjoy the companionship and support of teamwork, they also want recognition for their individual contribution. One of the most challenging tasks for any team leader is to create an environment where individuals can feel a sense of personal achievement, and are offered a degree of challenge and responsibility consistent with their ability. In order to remain motivated, individuals need to feel that their achievements are recognized and that they are making a valuable contribution within the team.

Obviously, it is in the team leader's best interests to ensure that all team members are encouraged in this way, since a dissatisfied individual can place a tremendous strain on team relationships and can have a detrimental effect on team achievements.

Knowing individuals

In order to develop each member of her team the teacher needs to get to know each one as an individual – to find out about particular interests and skills, and also about the parts of their work which they are most and least confident about.

This finding out process involves firstly discovering how each individual sees her role within the team. Nursery nurses may see their role differently depending on when they completed their training, and it would be inadvisable for the teacher to make assumptions based on her view of what she wants from a nurse. While keeping in mind the support she would like, the skilled teacher negotiates responsibilities based on each nursery nurse's perceptions of the role and on their ability to undertake that role.

For example, in one nursery team slightly different responsibilities were negotiated for each nursery nurse in relation to their involvement in recordkeeping. All staff agreed that they had a contribution to make to the process of recording children's progress, but it was clear that they would feel most comfortable with different approaches to the task. It was decided that one would keep a notebook of observations to contribute to the children's records, because she felt confident that her training had equipped her well to do this and because she enjoyed this aspect of her work. The other, who had trained many years ago when the NNEB training had placed less emphasis on the educational side of a child's development and on written recording, did not feel confident about writing observations but was keen to make a contribution to the children's records. She felt she was particularly sensitive to children's emotional needs and picked up on things which other staff sometimes missed. She was encouraged by the teacher to share her observations verbally, and to tick off evidence of children's interests and achievements on a checklist the teacher prepared. In this way the different strengths of both were valued, and both continued to feel they had an important contribution to make.

Appraising individuals

Just as the building of a team requires regular meetings, getting to know individuals can only be achieved through regular one-to-one discussions that focus on particular skills and interests, feelings about work and specific needs, such as training needs. These discussions can help team members review their own achievements to date and plan future developments, as well as providing the nursery teacher with an opportunity to acknowledge things done well and discuss any areas of concern.

Staff appraisal has become a more accepted part of school life and these discussions have been formalized in some schools. Just as the teacher is appraised by the headteacher of the school, so the nursery nurse is provided with opportunities to discuss her work with the teacher. This can take the form of a termly or half-termly meeting where both parties could identify and comment on:

- Particular areas of responsibility, i.e. those held currently, and new areas of responsibility for the future.
- Work that has gone well/been particularly enjoyable.
- Work that has not gone so well/not been so enjoyable.
- Relationships that have been most and least positive, i.e. with colleagues, children and parents.
- Particular strengths and weaknesses (using answers to the above to provide clues).
- Support (both human and training) needed to develop practice.
- Plans for the next few months.

These meetings should always be regarded as an opportunity for mutual review. It is just as important for the team member to be able to say what she needs from the leader as vice versa. Discussions of this kind can go a long way towards ensuring that the skills of each member of the team are developed and used to the full. Offering individuals positive feedback on their work within the team is a vital part of the teacher's responsibilities.

When individuals know that their strengths are recognized it is so much less threatening for them to acknowledge, and ask for support in tackling, their weaknesses.

Delegating responsibility

Once she knows the strengths of each member of her team it is often possible for the nursery teacher to delegate responsibility for some areas of work. For example, the nursery nurse who is particularly knowledgeable about gardening could be given responsibility for advising the other staff on developing the nursery outdoor area. This responsibility could involve ordering equipment as well as leading a session on planning what needs to be done, when and how. Because the ultimate responsibility for what happens in the nursery is still held by the teacher, it is essential that this work is carried out in consultation with her – it is important that the nursery nurse who has been given responsibility is encouraged to keep the teacher fully informed about all developments. Delegation does not mean off-loading! Neither does it mean allowing people to take responsibility by default and 'justifying' it afterwards – as in the case of the school secretary who was allowed to handle admissions to the nursery class single-handedly with no regard to school policy because 'she does it so well it would be a shame to take it away from her'. This approach to delegation often masks a real fear of tackling the school secretary!

Effective delegation means allowing someone else to use their skills, but this must be within the philosophical framework already established for the team, and must involve the support of the team leader.

Summarizing the Leadership Task

In summary, the three main areas of activity for the nursery teacher are:

1. Ensuring the tasks for which she is responsible are identified and achieved.
2. Developing a team approach and a shared sense of purpose.
3. Attending to the individual needs of team members.

So far we have focused mainly on how the nursery teacher acts in relation to her basic team, since this is the foundation on which nursery education is based. If this foundation is strong, all members of the basic team will be well equipped to include and involve parents, colleagues, governors, and students as part of the wider team.

Of course, it is not possible to approach leadership of the wider team in quite the same way, but the general principles remain the same. In other words, the aim of the teacher is to extend the shared sense of purpose and commitment to all members of the school community in order to enable others to understand and become involved in the children's education.

Personal Qualities of the Leader

It will be clear that although effective leadership depends on the teacher's understanding of what her task involves, there is also a personal dimension – in other words, it is not just what the leader does it is also the way that she does it (Stubbs, 1985).

During an in-service course, a group of experienced nursery teachers and nursery nurses were asked to think about themselves as people who are led and to consider the question: What makes an effective leader? It was clear from their replies that they consider the experience and personal style of the leader to be extremely influential. They identified a number of attributes which they considered essential for effective leadership.

Commitment and enthusiasm

Leaders must be committed to and enthusiastic about their work so that they can inspire other members of the team. They need a positive, cheerful attitude to their work and should have a sense of humour so that work remains a pleasure for all concerned. An outgoing personality was considered to be essential.

Ability to deal with others

Leaders need to be 'caring and kind but firm'. They should be patient and should trust others to give of their best. Positive attitudes towards the contribution made by others are very important. If the nursery teacher expects very little from 'staff, parents, etc. like these' she will get very little from them.

Effective leaders must have good observation skills so that they can tune into team relationships, recognize achievements and can give positive feedback to the individual(s) concerned.

Good communication skills

This is probably the most important of all the skills required of the team leader. The leadership role requires teachers to project themselves and set the standard for the class – it requires them to take the lead and to make things happen. They can only do this if they communicate with their team. It is essential that they listen to others and are receptive to their suggestions or advice, explain their own ideas clearly, and challenge sensitively and tactfully.

Consistency and a sense of fairness

Leaders must be seen to be fair and consistent in their dealings with all members of the team. There should not be one set of rules for some and another set for others. This requires leaders to have the courage of their convictions and to be able to tackle difficult situations sensitively but firmly at times. If leaders are able to demonstrate these personal qualities they are much more likely to win the respect of their team.

Loyalty to the team

Leaders should put the team's interests first. They should act or speak authoritatively on the team's behalf and should not be a 'yes person'. This is particularly important for teachers working in primary schools where the need to represent the interests of very young children is most important and can be most difficult. Team members must feel that their leader will stand up for their principles and not be swayed by others outside the team who may be advocating an approach inconsistent with these principles. For example, a speech therapist who was meeting with a teacher to negotiate a language programme for a child with communication difficulties, advocated the use of some pictures which were old fashioned and were inconsistent with the nursery team's clearly written antisexist policy. It was the teacher's responsibility to explain tactfully why these pictures were not appropriate and to offer suggestions for more suitable resources from the school stock. In doing this it was, of course, essential that the teacher made it clear that it was the pictures and not the ideas for working with the child which were inappropriate.

Ability to earn respect by example

At a basic level the team leader needs to provide a model of good attendance, punctuality and hard work, since a team will usually adjust its behaviour to match the leader's apparent expectations. If the teacher takes time off for every minor ailment and/or regularly arrives late, then very soon other members of the team will be doing the same. It is difficult for the leader to retain respect in this situation.

All team members need to feel that their leader possesses some skills, knowledge and experience which the rest of the team do not have. It is expected that the leader will be well informed and will be able to act as a role model through example. Team members need to see the leader putting principles into action and being able to explain clearly the links between theory and practice. This is never more important than when parents or students are involved in working with the children. In this situation, the skilled nursery teacher offers opportunities for others to watch her in action with a group of children, after which she will talk about what she was hoping to achieve and comment on what actually took place.

Ms M., a parent of one of the nursery children, had asked to help in the classroom for an hour one morning. She had never done this before and was unsure about what she could offer. The teacher had an informal chat with her first thing in the morning and suggested that she should play Kim's game with a small group of children to encourage memory and talk. The teacher emphasized the value of having extra adults to talk with the children, and demonstrated the game which involves collecting a small number of items – in this case a small yellow car, a plastic animal, a red pencil, a brown and white feather and a small, wooden house from a construction kit – and a cloth big enough to cover the items. The teacher encouraged the children to count the number of items and talk about each one in detail. She then covered the items with the cloth and took one away without the children seeing what it was. She then asked them to say what was missing. After a couple more demonstration sessions the teacher briefly explained how Ms M. could continue the game, emphasizing the importance of encouraging talk and giving her some ideas for making the game more challenging as the children gained experience, e.g. by adding more items (perhaps another different coloured pencil), taking more than one item away, choosing individual children to take the items away and so on.

Because of the teacher's informative and reassuring modelling of the game, Ms M. was able to work confidently with the children – she was very soon thinking up her own ideas for developing the children's interest in the activity. Above all, she thoroughly enjoyed her first experience of helping at the nursery and gained some insight into the school's aims and objectives in the process. She was very eager to find time to come again. Without the nursery teacher's support she might have felt a bit like a spare part and might have been reluctant to repeat the experience.

Self-Evaluation

It is difficult to separate inherent, personal qualities from those qualities which can be gained through experience and practice. However, it is clear that nursery teachers, if they are to develop confidently their leadership skills, need to be able to review their personal and interpersonal skills as well as their practice.

This has obvious implications for initial teacher training. When selecting students the future role of the nursery teacher as leader of adults should be taken into account. If, for example, good communication skills are needed to take on this role, then these should be assessed at interview, and opportunities should be given to evaluate and develop these further throughout the course. Many teachers feel they would have benefited greatly from assertiveness training courses, and there seems to be no reason why this kind of experience could not be included in initial training courses.

Similarly, tutors on initial and in-service courses need to act as role models for their students, and offer a responsive, facilitative, reflective approach to training rather than the didactic approach which sometimes dominates. An example of this didactic approach to training was given by a newly qualified nursery teacher during a discussion on young children's ability to make choices. She told how her college tutor had insisted that only one type of drawing implement (e.g. wax crayons or coloured pencils) should be offered to children at any one time. When asked by other members of the discussion group to explain why, she was unable to do so and became visibly anxious. Her college experience had not prepared her well for helping colleagues to develop principles for practice – at least on this issue. No doubt her college tutor had a reason, but tutors should realize that many of their dogmatic statements will be remembered but the reason for them forgotten! However tempting it may be to tell teachers what to do, in the long term it is always more productive to support them in thinking and reasoning through the issues for themselves.

If teachers are to encourage and support their team they need to be encouraged and supported themselves, and need to be given the skills to enable them to work effectively with other adults. They need to see these skills being demonstrated, and discussed by others.

Leadership Challenges

Nursery teachers very rarely have non-contact time (i.e. time away from their class teaching responsibilities) available to them, and have equally rarely received training in leadership skills. Given that the role of the leader is a time-consuming and highly skilled one, it is hardly surprising that some teachers run into difficulties. Indeed, it is to the credit of all nursery teachers that they cope as well as they do!

The previously mentioned group of teachers identified four main areas of difficulty when they were asked to consider the question: What is difficult about leading?

Fear and lack of confidence

This can be 'paralysing' and can discourage the teacher from trying to tackle her leadership role. Inexperienced teachers and those new to a particular situation were most likely to be affected by this difficulty. With the current shortage of early years trained teachers the number of teachers without an appropriate training working with nursery children is increasing. These teachers are particularly vulnerable because they are often less aware of the needs of young children than the nursery nurses they have been appointed to lead.

The overwhelming nature of the job

This is characterized by having too much to do in too little time. Many teachers feel this leads them to have excessively high expectations of themselves and of others. There are also situations where other team members are unwilling to become involved in all aspects of nursery work, increasing the burden on the teacher, e.g. the nursery nurse who does not see why she should contribute to the children's records and refuses to do so. Thankfully these cases are rare, and it is important to note that sometimes it is the nursery teacher who asks too little of her extremely skilled nursery nurses. Disputes of this kind have emphasized the need for clear contracts of employment for all staff involved.

This problem was highlighted again when the five in-service days for teachers were introduced. Some nursery nurses, who work to a different contract, felt they should not be expected to fulfil what were essentially the teachers' contractual obligations. Clearly a team approach requires joint opportunities for training, and in some areas this issue has been resolved by way of a pay rise which took into account the extra demands being made on nursery nurses. However, in some areas it is felt that team relationships were damaged at least temporarily by the dispute.

Above all, this situation provided an opportunity for nursery staff to explain to others the unique interdependence of their roles, and has increased demand for other opportunities for joint training. The five in-service days were not a problem (at least not in this way!) for other teachers.

Fear of unpopularity

Most human beings want to be liked and to please others and want to receive positive feedback from the people they work with – particularly when they work in close proximity with others as nursery staff do. Some teachers admit that their greatest fear is being disliked by other members of their team, and that they let this fear prevent them from tackling difficult issues, or encourage them to 'ignore' practice which is inconsistent with their aims. Either of these reponses can lead to resentment in the long term.

Handling conflict

This is closely related to fear of unpopularity. Often fear is caused by the difficulties involved in dealing with differences of opinion or in handling conflict. Lack of time is also given as a reason why conflict is so difficult to deal with. Often a tactful, considered response is required and yet the leader is sometimes expected to respond immediately before she has had time to think the issue through fully. Having to respond before her own mind is clear often leads to an inappropriate reaction, which can cause even more difficulties. Little wonder then that conflict is often avoided.

Dealing with personalities

Any situation involving a number of personalities will inevitably present challenges. Teachers of older children usually only have to tolerate those adult personalities they find most difficult during breaks and staff meetings. However, the nursery staff spend most of their time together and it would be naïve to ignore the fact that there have been situations where two or more quite incompatible personalities have been placed together. Teachers, aware as they are of the need to present a united front to parents and children, go to great lengths to minimize differences but there is no doubt that this can cause considerable stress.

In addition to their immediate colleagues, teachers are also expected to involve parents from a wide range of backgrounds and cultures in their work. They will find some of these parents easier to work with than others, but will recognize their responsibility to them all.

Tackling the Challenges

Making the job manageable

Most nursery teachers would agree that leading the team gets easier with practice. They would also agree that mistakes will be made and that these mistakes provide powerful learning experiences. It is clear that some of the difficulties described above can be resolved, at least to some extent, through understanding the tasks involved in leadership. This understanding will not give the teacher more hours in the day, but it will give her the confidence to put some tasks to one side while she and the team concentrate on others. If the rest of the team feel they have a specific goal which they can work towards and, most importantly, achieve, they too will be more likely to make an effort.

Similarly, individual team members will be encouraged to give of their best if they are offered the chance to take some responsibilty for an aspect of work which particularly interests them and for which they have specific skills.

Through working together with a shared philosophy, towards clearly identified aims and objectives, all members of the basic team can gain the confidence to articulate their work to others, thereby relieving the teacher of some of the responsibility for communication. In this way she still retains responsibility but does not have to do it all herself.

Making time for leadership

This will always be the central problem for nursery teachers. There is unlikely ever to be as much time for leadership as they would wish. Accepting this and refusing to use the shortage of time as an excuse for inactivity is one step towards tackling the problem.

Nursery staff have particular difficulties as far as making time to meet together is concerned. They are on duty with the children virtually all the time they are in school. Those who offer full-time places do not even get common lunch breaks since one member of staff is on duty while the other has a break.

In spite of these difficulties, nursery staff do find time to meet together informally and formally to discuss their work. Some teams, having organized the learning environment in such a way that minimal setting up is necessary in the mornings (for details see Chapter 3), use this time to talk together. Others have a regular team meeting one afternoon each week at the end of the school day. Those who have common lunch breaks use this time to talk with each other – in some schools headteachers enable lunchtime meetings to take place by relieving staff of meals supervision one day a week. Headteachers benefit from this arrangement, too, since they get to know the full-time nursery children.

Having established a regular time for the team to meet it is essential that the teacher takes responsibilty for ensuring that the most effective use is made of this time. Many teachers write a weekly sheet (or page in a book) of news and items of general interest, such as visitors to the school, etc., for their teams so that weekly meetings are not taken up with basic information giving.

Formal meetings can therefore be carefully planned to cover the priorities the team have identified. One person – usually but not always the nursery teacher – ensures the team stays on task and allocates time sensibly so that they achieve their aims for each meeting. Progress may be slow in these circumstances but it will happen nevertheless.

Making time to communicate with the wider team presents an even greater challenge. Being available to talk with parents in the mornings and at the end of the session requires a routine which frees some staff from supervising children at these times of the day. If all staff are involved with story groups at the end of the session they will not be able to talk to parents. The nursery team need to consider how they organize the nursery day to provide themselves with opportunities to communicate with others. Headteachers responsible for nursery classes must also be helped to recognize the importance of establishing this wider network in order that they view requests for non-contact time or additional staffing sympathetically. It is clearly not possible for nursery teachers to involve parents, governors and other professionals in the team's work effectively without some support of this kind.

Whether or not she is given any extra time, the teacher as leader of the team needs to organize her own time as effectively as possible. She is the role model for her team and needs to be seen to be doing her job efficiently. She will always have an enormous number of different things to do and to think about. One way of ensuring that everything is done is to make a list in a notebook of things which have to be done each week, adding to it as the week goes by. By numbering the tasks in order of priority or urgency and crossing them off when they are accomplished, she can gain control of her workload and resist the temptation to flit from one task to another without completing any of them. She can also see clearly whether or not it is possible to fit in an additional task which is being asked of her.

Lack of time will always be a problem for teachers, but there are always ways of making better use of the time that is available. Indeed, the most effective teachers pack so much into each day, that they have much to teach their primary and secondary colleagues about time management!

Coping with fear, lack of confidence and conflict

It is clear from comments made by nursery teachers that leading the team can be a very lonely part of their job which generates considerable self-doubt and anxiety. To a certain extent confidence comes from getting to grips with the leadership task, but this does not account for the fear which comes from personal and interpersonal dimensions. Nursery teachers have identified and developed a number of ways of building up their confidence and counteracting the loneliness of their role.

Developing support networks

Having other nursery teachers to talk to is essential, since only they have an intimate understanding of the role. Many teachers use in-service courses as an opportunity to meet others of like mind – tutors need to bear this in mind and build in opportunities for discussion. Other teachers – mainly in towns and cities – have established informal local groups which meet regularly to provide a forum for nursery staff in the area to discuss issues of mutual interest. Others have established telephone contact with other nursery teachers. All of these opportunities provide an invaluable lifeline when things are proving difficult. Sharing the problem with someone else is often the best way of finding the beginnings of a solution – but that someone else needs to understand the issues!

Developing awareness of strengths and weaknesses

Teachers realize that they can gain confidence from an awareness of their own strengths. It is easy to dwell on weaknesses and never identify the things which are done well: this applies to oneself as well as to colleagues. An ability to recognize both strengths and weaknesses is essential to effective team work. By concentrating on the strengths of all members of the team it is possible to establish a positive base on which to build. Weaknesses can then be seen in the context of already established strengths. The teacher often finds herself protecting her team from the criticisms of the outside world, e.g. 'Yes, I acknowledge that the music experiences we are offering at the moment are not very exciting, but we have recently worked very hard at encouraging the children's language and literacy development and I believe this is a real strength because . . .'. In this way she prevents her team and herself from becoming overwhelmed by the enormity of their task.

Gaining respect

Successful teachers recognize that they must gain the respect of their team and that this does not necessarily mean being popular. They know that there are times when they will have to make a stand, and that a certain amount of conflict is inevitable when people work in close contact with each other. They also know that adults are often not as good as children at expressing their feelings and thoughts, and that a great deal of guess work and investigation is involved in identifying difficulties within the team.

Analysing problems as they come up rather than pretending they do not exist is the best way of getting to the root of the difficulty and finding a method for dealing with it. Nursery teachers spend a considerable amount of their time observing, listening and acting as evaluators. It is just as important that they evaluate what adults are doing and saying as it is that they observe and listen to the children.

They need to ask regularly questions such as 'Why did S. do that?', 'What could I do to help K. understand that?', 'Why did M. answer so abruptly when I asked her that?', 'Did B. really mean what she just said or was she trying to make a point about something else?' and so on. This kind of analysis of the situation is vital if an appropriate reaction is to be identified. It is never a good idea to respond on the spur of the moment without allowing some thinking time. This will sometimes mean saying to a team member 'I'm sorry but I can't discuss that at the moment, but I would like to talk to you about it after school or tomorrow morning'. Gaining time in this way can prevent outbursts which are later regretted, or an embarrassed avoidance of the situation.

Stubbs (1985, p. 26) describes the traditional responses to conflict and difficulty as:

. fight (aggression)
flight (avoidance)
or resentful submission (accommodation)

He suggests assertive behaviour, where all parties are enabled to retain their self-esteem, as an alternative response. This approach relies on leaders being honest with all team members right from the start and should lead to an atmosphere of mutual respect.

This honesty requires the leader to be able to admit to any mistakes she has made rather than becoming defensive in the face of criticism. Often unco-operative behaviour by a nursery nurse is a way of expressing dissatisfaction with the way the teacher has treated her – perhaps she feels angry because she was not consulted or involved in a change the teacher has made. It is up to the teacher to find an opportunity to ask if she has done or said anything to upset the nursery nurse (rather than assuming the nursery nurse is at fault) and to gently persist until the problem has been aired. It is then equally essential that the nursery teacher apologizes for any wrong she has done. Very few people can resist an apology and a genuine attempt to put things right. If the nursery nurse continues to behave uncooperatively, the teacher may need to take further action and gain the support of the headteacher, but this is very much a last resort after the nursery teacher has identified and attempted to make up for any wrong on her part. If the problem is not resolved in this kind of way, the team will be unable to move forward in harmony and the teacher's role as leader will continue to be undermined.

If the teacher is able to accept that she can make mistakes, but that these mistakes can be rectified through an honest approach, she will be well equipped to tackle the challenges of leadership. Ultimately she will also gain the respect of her colleagues – a much more valuable commodity than popularity. If they see that their leader is able to openly discuss her anxieties and mistakes, they will also feel encouraged to be open about their grievances.

Experienced teachers agree that however frightening at the time it may be to deal with conflict, it always seems less so after the event, and it is always a relief to have done something positive, rather than to have used fear as an excuse for inaction.

Asking for help

Nursery teachers recognize that there are occasions when they will need to ask for help from those with greater authority than themselves. The headteacher is there to offer leadership to the teacher and can be called on to help with particularly difficult problems. One day, a child in a nursery class was called for by a very drunk father who was in no state to look after a 3-year-old. The teacher explained to the father that she could not allow the child to go home alone with him, but was unable to get the point across. She felt unable to take sole responsibility for the situation, and that she would have to involve the primary headteacher in deciding what was to be done. So she took the father over to the headteacher's office for the decision to be reached.

Similarly, a teacher may ask the headteacher to arbitrate in a situation where there is a dispute about the duties of a team member. A nursery nurse was persistently late, and continued to be so even after the teacher had reminded her that her contract required her to be in school in time to help set up the nursery environment. The headteacher was asked to clarify the situation for the nursery nurse.

In the case of personality clashes, it is often valuable to be able to talk to an outsider with greater experience who can bring a less subjective perspective to the situation and may even act as arbitrator in extreme circumstances. An experienced nursery nurse felt the nursery teacher in her class undermined her by not communicating effectively with her. The teacher felt she had tried to communicate, but that the nursery nurse always responded negatively. The point had been reached where working relationships had become strained and there seemed to be no way forward. They both agreed to a meeting in the presence of the headteacher, who was able to support them both through the process of realizing how an initial failure on the part of the teacher to include the nursery nurse in her plan to invite parents to borrow books from the nursery library, had led to resentment which was now being characterized by the nursery nurse's uncooperative attitude. Both members of staff could see that they had some responsibility for the current situation and that there were aspects of each personality which annoyed the other. As a result of the meeting they were able to establish a more positive working relationship, and were subsequently more able to talk openly about problems as they arose.

As in any close relationship it is vital that grievances are aired as they arise and not allowed to blow up out of all proportion. This requires all parties involved in nursery education to behave in a mature, responsible and open manner. While this can be expected of, but not necessarily achieved by, paid trained staff it cannot always be expected of parents who are motivated primarily by their interest in their own child. The parent of the child who had been bitten by another child, will not always be able to respond calmly to the teacher's attempts at reassurance. The same parent's angry promise that she will find the perpetrator of the 'crime' and punish him or her is understandable but not at all easy for the teacher to handle.

There is no single easy method for coping with the unpredictable, daily demands of the people the teacher has to cope with. One thing is clear though: the more effective she has been in involving everyone in her work and encouraging them all to work together for the benefit of all the children, the less likely it is that serious conflict will arise. Many of the conflict situations which arise can be predicted and can be prepared for and defused in advance. All nursery teachers know that it is likely that a child will be bitten sometime. With this knowledge they and their teams can think about how they could prevent this happening, and how they could deal with it if it did happen. They might also think about how they could share with parents the possibility of something like this happening to their child. Being well prepared removes at least some of the anxiety from conflict situations.

Positive Aspects of Leadership

The leadership role makes considerable demands on the nursery teacher. There are times when working in a team seems like a mixed blessing, or when it seems as if everyone is making demands at once. However, being a leader of a nursery team has its positive side which will have been apparent throughout earlier sections of this chapter, and it is important not to lose sight of this.

Nursery teachers benefit greatly from having other adults to try out ideas on, and to challenge their thinking. Having to explain and defend their views to others from a variety of backgrounds in a clear, accessible way, prevents the nursery teacher from becoming complacent and stale. It keeps her mind working and her ideas flowing. Those teachers who have also taught infants often say how much they missed this challenge to their thinking when they were working alone with the children in an infant class.

Working with other people who have all trained to work with young children provides many opportunities for learning together. All members of the team have something unique to offer and each one, including the leader, can learn from and offer support and companionship to the others. Above all, the nursery team can have fun together. They all know the same group of children and can delight together in the daily happenings. Teachers and their teams value enormously the time spent together at the beginning and end of each day when anecdotes are shared and plans made. These informal get togethers provide the leader with a firm foundation from which the more formal aspects of her leadership duties can develop.

The themes which have been introduced in this chapter will be explored further throughout the book. In the following chapters the importance of clear principles, team work and respect for individuals will be emphasized. This is because the nursery teacher approaches all aspects of her work as the leader of the team. Her effectiveness in all the other roles she has to adopt is influenced by her effectiveness as a leader. This should be fully recognized by those who offer training in nursery education.

Some Points for Discussion

Assessing Leadership Skills

Who leads? Think about all the people you come into contact with in the course of your work and make a list of all those people who lead you (or offer you support) and all those you are expected to lead (offer support to).

When do you lead? List all the situations during the last week or so when you have been expected to take on a leadership role.

When are you led? Make a list of all the situations during the last week or so when you have been led.

What is an effective leader? Using your lists think of some of the situations where you have been well led/supported and make a list of the leadership qualities you think are most important or effective. Ask yourself:

- When and by whom was I led well? Why was this person's leadership effective?
- How did I feel about my work when I was led well?
- Could I have done anything to help the person leading me to lead more effectively? (Think about any times when you did not feel you were led well and try to identify anything you could have done to make the leader's role easier.)

Answering these questions should give you some insight into what it feels like to be led, which you can relate to feelings of the people you lead.

What Kind of a Leader are You?

Next, think about yourself as a leader of other adults and (using your lists) ask yourself:

- In which situations did I lead effectively?
- What reasons do I have for considering I was effective?
- Why was I able to lead effectively in these situations and with these people?
- In which situations and with which people did I not lead effectively? Why?
- What was difficult about these situations/people? Did I do (or not do) something which made the situation more difficult? Can I trace the difficulties back to a failure to pay attention to any of the tasks of leadership outlined in this chapter, e.g. a failure to establish a shared sense of purpose, or a lack of understanding by colleagues that they need to work as a team?

- What could I do to make this kind of situation easier next time?
- In which leadership situations do I feel most/least confident? How can I increase my confidence?

Imagine members of your team were describing you as a leader – what do you think they would say about you? What would you say about your own leadership style? What are your strengths and weaknesses?

What Kind of Personal Qualities do you bring to Leadership?

- How would you describe your own personality? Which aspects of your own personality help you to be a leader? Which aspects hinder you?
- How would you assess your own ability to communicate your work/ beliefs to others? Which parts of your work do you communicate most/ least competently and why?
- How do you respond in potential conflict situations? Think about actual situations you have had to deal with and how you responded, e.g. a parent aggressively challenges you to explain why her child needs to use sand. (The parent understandably considers sand a nuisance because it gets in the child's hair.) Were you defensive? Aggressive? Calm? Confident you could cope?
- In which situations are you most confident/least confident? How could you increase your confidence in all leadership situations? What support might you need?
- Is there a personality clash between you and another member of the team? Can you identify the cause(s) of this clash? (You may need to think back to trace what started the problem.) What could you do to improve the relationship? (This will require you to recognize your own responsibility for the clash.)

How can you Make Time for Leadership?

- List the time you spend engaged in formal and informal leadership activities. Is the balance between formal and informal about right, or do you need to make more opportunities for formal meetings of the team or of you and individuals? When could you find this time? (You will need to consider *not* doing some things to make time for this, and may consider asking for support from your headteacher.)
- Is the time you spend on leadership activities used effectively? (If you have a meeting of the basic team are you and the team clear about what you are to achieve, or does the meeting just ramble on?)

- When did you last find time to acknowledge the achievements of members of your team or talk to them individually about their work? How could you make more opportunities for this?
- How can you find time to communicate your work to the wider team (including parents) and listen to their views?

How can you get Support?

- What support is currently available to you in your leadership role?
- What support would you like/do you need?
- What steps have you taken or could you take to get this support? For example, start a self-help group with other nursery teachers, ask for training courses, talk to the headteacher and so on.
- Finally, what steps have you taken to help others understand the complexity of the nursery teacher's leadership role? Have you encouraged the local authority to invite experienced nursery teachers to talk to probationers about the leadership role, and to provide ongoing training in leadership skills?

2
HELPING CHILDREN TO FEEL 'AT HOME'

The Care and Education Debate

The separate funding and administration of care and education services for under-5s in Britain has resulted in considerable debate about what constitutes high quality provision for young children. The younger the children the more vulnerable and dependent on adults they are, and the greater their need for care and supervision. Traditionally, it has been expected that this need for care will be met within the family, but with the demographic changes which have prompted the government to consider how more women with children might be encouraged back into the workforce, and the growing number of parents who have to work to survive financially, there has been a gradual realization that a range of childcare facilities must be made available.

There is also considerable evidence that the period from birth to 5 years of age is a time when rapid intellectual development takes place, and that children at this stage are particularly receptive learners (Brierley, 1984). It is therefore vital that they have access to a high quality educational experience at this time.

The report of the Education, Science and Arts Committee (ESAC, 1989, p. viii) concluded that 'care and education for the under fives are complementary and inseparable'. It is therefore hard to understand why in this country there has been no real attempt by government to establish a properly funded, co-ordinated service for young children, which offers parents the child-care facilities they need, while at the same time giving high priority to the children's need for appropriate educational experiences.

Perhaps it is because young children's need for education as well as for care is still underestimated. The Rumbold Committee (DES, 1990, p. ii) claim that 'education for the under-fives can happen in a wide variety of settings', and use the term 'educator' to describe 'an adult working with the under-fives'. The inference that anyone, however minimally trained, can teach, would be totally unacceptable if applied to the education of older children. Why is there resistance to the idea that young children who are at a vulnerable stage in their development, also need appropriately trained teachers?

Is it because of the low status of those working with young children – the idea that because 3- and 4-year-olds are little anyone can educate them? Perhaps it is the care element which gets in the way of a full understanding of what is involved in working effectively with young children. It is quite possible for people with or without training to care about and for children. However, it requires highly trained staff to combine an appropriate education with this care. When inadequately trained staff try to educate the under-5s, what seems to happen is that the care element gets lost, and a transmission model of education takes over, curriculum content taking precedence over individual needs.

Research on 4-year-olds attending reception classes in primary schools with inappropriately trained teachers, has repeatedly demonstrated how children can rapidly become resentful and unhappy if their social and emotional needs are not met (Barrett, 1986; Bennett and Kell, 1989; NFER/SCDC, 1987). This is why training is so important. Only if the needs of the under-5s are fully understood, can an appropriate education be defined and developed. ESAC (1989, p. xxiii) were in no doubt that 'where the quality of education was of a high standard, one or more appropriately qualified teachers were on the staff'. It urged the DES and LEAs to find ways of giving higher status to nursery teachers. The members of this committee recognized that nursery trained teachers are well equipped to provide the combination of care and education which young children need. This chapter will demonstrate how the nursery teacher uses her knowledge of the developmental needs of 3- to 5-year-olds to establish an appropriate ethos and learning environment for them.

What Do Young Children Need?

Blenkin and Kelly (1987, p. 11) argue strongly that 'the prime concern of education should be to develop to the maximum the potential of every

child to function as a human being'. Their view of 'education as development' (p. 1) is common to most early-years trained teachers. It is in their
first few years at school (whether nursery or infant) that children must
learn to function as a member of a large social group outside the family,
and must develop the resources they need to cope with the emotional,
physical and intellectual challenges they will meet as they grow older.
Nursery trained teachers, in particular, understand their role in supporting
this all-round development and they know that the support they need to
offer will vary for each child.

This is because within any group of 3- and 4-year-olds there are wide
variations in development and maturity. All parents know how rapidly
children grow and develop during the first five years of their life. If they
have more than one child, they also know that no two children do the same
things at exactly the same age. These variations are usually quite normal,
but they require the nursery teacher to get to know and relate to children
as individuals and not as a group, and to be able to identify any unusual
variations in development which may require specialist help for the child.

When considering what young children need, the teacher therefore has
to observe and get to know each individual. Through a consideration of
two children attending the same nursery class we can see how the teacher
needs to apply her general knowledge of 3- to 5-year-olds to the specific
needs of individuals. The following outlines are based on a review of the
progress of these children towards the end of their first term.

Natalie and John had settled well and were enthusiastic, well-motivated
members of the class. They came from the same council estate and lived in
small maisonettes in low rise blocks. Both had attended day care provision
before joining the nursery class and Natalie was still cared for during parts
of the day by a childminder. Both children attended nursery full time.

Natalie (who was 3 years old when admitted) was a tall, physically well-
developed child. She was very independent in dressing, toileting herself
and eating lunch and strongly resisted any help offered. She was a confident user of the nursery environment. She selected a broad range of
opportunities for herself both in and out of doors, but her favourite activity
was home corner play. She spent a great deal of time in this area and
particularly enjoyed using the telephone. She could often be seen standing
with one foot up on a chair (or even the ironing board on one occasion) and
one hand on her hip, having a lengthy and usually very loud 'conversation'.
It was impossible to understand more than the occasional word. Natalie's
language consisted of one or two recognizable words and a considerable
amount of 'babble' of the kind most usually associated with children of a
much younger age. She was able to imitate very expressively the intonation

patterns involved in a conversation on the telephone. When trying to communicate with adults and other children in the nursery, she became very frustrated because she was unable to express anything other than very basic needs in a way that others could understand. This was extremely difficult for her because she was by nature a sociable child who wanted very much to join in and share her own experiences with others. Occasionally her frustration led to severe temper tantrums.

John (3 years 10 months when admitted) on the other hand was a quiet, gentle, articulate child. He was also very capable of attending to his own physical needs but he was less confident about making use of the nursery environment. He sometimes seemed nervous of the other children, particularly the more boisterous ones, and was unable to stand his ground if another child challenged him for a piece of equipment – in these situations he would let the other child have the toy and move quickly away from the area. Most of all John liked to look at books, preferably while cuddling up to an adult. He could 'read' simple repetitive stories such as *Where's Spot?* (Hill, 1980) and *Bears in the Night* (Berenstain, 1981) and was interested in discussing the words in books. During one story telling session with a teacher he asked 'Where does it say but?' There were one or two children in the group who John enjoyed playing imaginative games with, but he was always watchful of those other children he seemed to consider to be a threat.

It is clear that the needs of these two children are quite different. Most nursery classes contain children like them plus many others at various stages of development. Helping these, and the other twenty-four or more children in her group, reach their full potential will stretch the nursery teacher and her team to the limit. In Chapter 5 we look at meeting these needs on an individual basis. Although in this chapter we focus on the general needs of young children, the developmental variations within a group make it essential for the nursery teacher to consider the specific individual needs of each child she works with.

The role of carer and educator of young children requires the teacher to consider each child as a whole person and to attend to the total needs of each one. It is debatable whether any teacher should focus on academic attainment without considering other needs, but it is certain that the nursery teacher should not. She knows that if she is to plan an appropriate curriculum for the children she must consider their social, emotional and physical needs, as well as their intellectual needs (DES, 1989a).

In the course of her work the teacher has to be aware of many different kinds of need. As she interacts with the children she operates at many different levels and may be responding to several different needs at once.

The various needs are considered separately in this chapter and the next to highlight the skill involved in developing the kind of ethos and environment which would promote this kind of development and learning.

The Need for Equality of Opportunity

Given the inequalities which exist at national and regional level, with less than a quarter of 3- and 4-year-olds gaining access to nursery education (January 1989 DES statistics), the idea that equality of opportunity can be achieved by nursery teachers may seem like a forlorn hope. But when we read in one study (Osborn and Milbank, 1987, p. 206) that 'as many as 46 per cent of the most disadvantaged children had received no form of pre-school education, compared with only 10 per cent of the most advantaged group', we begin to see that admission policies, over which teachers have some control, may be responsible for consolidating inequality.

Due to the limited number of state-funded nursery education places and the large numbers of children needing them, teachers and headteachers have considerable power to include or exclude children through their admission policies. They can decide whether they will give priority to particular groups of children, such as those with special needs, those with working parents, or those learning English as a second language. They can also decide to admit children strictly on a first come first served basis. If this second option is chosen, it is inevitable that some children, whose parents are unfamiliar with, or unable to cope with, the procedures, will be left out. Although the nursery teacher does not have sole responsibility for admission policies, she can have a tremendous influence on them. Her attitude can determine which children are considered positively.

Offering, as far as possible, equal access to nursery education is a start but it is not enough in itself. Having admitted children to nursery class, teachers have then to ensure that all children are given an equal chance to take advantage of the range of experiences on offer, and that all children feel equally valued as part of the group.

Teachers have been challenged over the last ten years or so to recognize that their own attitudes, policies and practices may discriminate against, and limit the opportunities of, some children because of their gender, class, cultural background, or special educational needs. This has been difficult for many teachers to accept, not least for nursery teachers, who sometimes used to claim that they treated 'all children the same', or that 'there is no racism or sexism in my nursery'.

These views stemmed from a belief that young children do not notice colour, and that nursery activities are used equally by both sexes. These beliefs have been strongly challenged by researchers. Milner (1975, 1983) demonstrated that young children do notice differences in skin colour, and that they attach value to these skin colours. The idea that nursery activities are equally available to girls and boys has also been challenged by, among others, Whyte (1983), who focused on the different ways boys and girls used the home corner, and by Thomas (1988), who worked with nursery and infant staff to discover and discuss the extent of sex stereotyping in their classes. Both studies show how children's ideas about gender are formed early, and that schools can unconsciously reinforce stereotypical views and behaviour.

It has also been shown that working class children can be disadvantaged within the nursery class. Tizard and Hughes (1984, p. 257) found that nursery staff often had low expectations of children from working class backgrounds putting these children 'at an educational disadvantage in school'.

Children with special educational needs are often admitted to mainstream nursery schools and classes (BAECE, 1990). Those with more obvious disabilities will usually have been assessed prior to school entry and additional support may have been made available. Often, however, a child's special educational needs are identified by the nursery staff. It is they who will have to act as advocates for the child and ensure that the support he or she needs is forthcoming. If children with special educational needs are to benefit from nursery education and not be unnecessarily limited, it is essential that appropriate, special provision is made for them.

All children need to feel proud of themselves and of their family. They need to feel valued for what they are and they need to feel competent and that they can achieve. They need to feel safe within the school environment, confident that they will not be bullied, nor subjected to racist or sexist taunts. But it is not just the victims of prejudice who need the support of the nursery teacher. She also has to help over-confident children, who seem to consider themselves to be superior to others, to develop the kind of positive identity which does not depend on demeaning others. Only if she works with the group of boys, who dominate certain activities or equipment and deny other children the opportunity to take part, can she ensure that girls will have equal access to the curriculum. Similarly a black child will only feel properly valued if he or she sees and hears the teacher confronting the child who has made a racist remark.

Working Towards Equality of Opportunity

The nursery teacher must consider her own attitudes and all aspects of her practice. Many teachers and their teams have begun to develop equal opportunities policies and, as they have done so, have realized that they are involved in developing a total educational philosophy. Work on equal opportunities is an integral part of curriculum development and has to affect people as well as resources. It is not enough to put chopsticks in the home corner – it is also essential that children know what they are, and how they are used. If a child makes a negative remark about Chinese food this must be confronted.

Only when teachers confront the difficult issues, rather than ignore them, can real progress be made towards equality of opportunity. Derman-Sparks (1989, p. x) acknowledges that 'it is not always easy to implement anti-bias curriculum on a regular basis'. She suggests that nursery staff need to be prepared to 'learn by doing: by making mistakes, and thinking about it, and trying again'. As leader of the team, the teacher has to demonstrate her commitment to positive action. She has to be prepared to tackle the incidents she notices herself, and those which others draw to her attention.

Taking this action is not easy. What, for example, is the best way of dealing with the 4-year-old child who has just told her black friend (who had announced proudly which infant school she was going to), that 'My mum says I can't go to that school, 'cos it's full of blacks'? Or, the best way of responding to the child's mother who, when told exactly what her child had said, replied 'Oh dear, she's got it all wrong. She *is* going to that school – it's . . . school which is full of blacks'?

This is the reality of tackling racism, and it is important to acknowledge the stress and anxiety felt by those trying to take positive action against it, as well the hurt caused to the victims of it. However, anxiety and hurt are considerably relieved for all concerned once action, however clumsy, has been taken. Skills in dealing with these difficult issues can only develop with practice, and the teacher who does not act because she believes she will not get it right, denies herself the opportunity to learn.

Similarly, an admission policy which offers places on a first come first served basis may be easier to administer, and appear quite fair, but will cause considerable stress to staff when they realize which children they have excluded – the child who has just moved into bed and breakfast accommodation in the area, or the child whose parents speak no English and did not know about registering early for a place, or the child with special educational needs. A policy which ensures that those children who most need nursery education get places may be more complicated to explain, but is much easier to live with in the long term.

Because they are in close contact with parents and children every day, teachers have many opportunities to hear and see evidence of the difficult issues mentioned above. Many of them have shown themselves willing to promote the concept of equality in all parts of their work. Often they have to discuss these difficult issues with those who hold different values and are resistent to their approach. Work on dealing with these issues is still at an early stage and many teachers are honest enough to admit that they often feel quite inadequate. How teachers demonstrate their commitment to equality of opportunity is examined in this and the next chapter, as part of the exploration of children's developmental needs.

The Need for Security

If you asked parents to describe what the nursery staff do to provide a secure environment for the children, and then asked nursery teachers the same question, the answers would probably reveal that each group interpreted the word 'security' differently. Parents are most likely to think about their child's physical safety: Is it possible to get out of the building or grounds? Are there any dangers such as sharp edges, low electrical sockets or climbing frames with no safety surface? Teachers are more likely to focus on the children's emotional security: What are the things which worry children about school life? How can we help the children to make the transition from home to school? How can we help Mark to be more assertive? This difference in perspective does not mean teachers are unaware of physical dangers, or that parents are not aware that their child may feel anxious when leaving the home environment: it merely highlights different initial reactions. Both kinds of security are obviously equally important to the young child.

The Need for Physical Security and Safety

Young children are usually unaware of the range of dangers in the environment. Because they are growing rapidly they are physically active and are generally delightfully keen to explore everything they come into contact with. This exploration involves touching, and often tasting, as well as the relatively safer looking and listening. They will not know that an interesting object can cut, or is poisonous or unhygienic. Neither are they necessarily aware that, if they throw this solid wooden brick like they just threw the sponge ball, it could hit another child and cause an injury. They are often quite ingenious at finding new ways of using objects and materials. Most parents and teachers know about the child who put a small piece of equipment up their nose or in their ear, or 'posted' something valuable down a drain!

Some of the equipment in the nursery class will be unfamiliar to the children and will require them to learn new skills. Climbing frames, wheeled toys, hammers and nails at the woodwork bench, scissors, large blocks and so on are all potentially dangerous, and children need opportunities to learn to use them without endangering themselves and others.

Particularly during their first few weeks at nursery school or class, some children will even try to go home. Parents have a right to expect that their small, vulnerable children will be protected from dangers of these kinds.

Ensuring Physical Security and Safety

Checking for health and safety hazards

Most schools are designed and regularly inspected for safety, and teachers are used to monitoring to ensure that no hazards have developed. In many nurseries, particularly in cities, an early morning check of the outside play area to remove any dangerous litter, which may have been thrown in, is part of the routine. All members of the team are aware of the need to check equipment regularly for broken parts and sharp edges, the kitchen and areas containing cleaning equipment are made inaccessible to children except when they are under staff supervision, such as when taking part in a cooking activity. Toilet and washing facilities are checked and kept as clean as possible, and the children are taught to wash their hands after toileting, before lunch and after handling pets.

The teacher must ensure that children are physically safe and that their health will not be endangered through poor standards of hygiene. However, nursery nurse training usually results in a much deeper understanding of health and safety issues than does teacher training, so often the nursery teacher will take the advice of her nursery nurse colleagues. This does not mean that all cleaning and checking is left to the nursery nurse. Routine tasks of this kind are the responsibility of all nursery staff, since they are too vital to the effective and safe functioning of the nursery to be left to one person. By encouraging the nursery nurse to use her skills, the teacher is maximizing the potential of the team.

Encouraging safe use of equipment

Helping children to develop the skills they need to use safely the entire range of nursery equipment, is given high priority. The philosophy of nursery education depends on high expectations of children, that is, a belief that children can behave responsibly if they are helped to understand how they are expected to behave and, more importantly, why they are being asked to behave in a particular way. One response to potentially dangerous equipment would be to keep it out of the nursery! It is to their credit that teachers usually reject this option.

In the best nursery schools and classes opportunities for woodwork, strenuous physical activity and involvement in projects, such as building a low garden wall, are regularly made available, and with well-planned adult support very young children develop skills which many adults would be proud of.

Sylvia (3 years and 9 months) was 'ironing' in the home corner in an open plan nursery school. The ironing board collapsed. Without reference to an adult, she picked it up, carried it to the woodwork bench (which was on the other side of the building) and mended it using a hammer and nail. She then carried it back to the home corner and continued ironing. She was able to do this because the teacher (a keen carpenter) had previously involved her in mending equipment, including the ironing board. This nursery teacher, as well as providing girls and boys with a model of a woman capable of doing what is often seen as male work, had very high expectations of the children. She taught them how to use equipment safely, explaining what could happen if they misused it, and then trusted them to behave responsibly. The children fulfilled her expectations. It saddens many nursery staff that the children's skills in these areas are not always encouraged and developed in the infant school.

Establishing safety rules

In order to make it possible to offer this kind of exciting, extending range of experiences to the children, many teachers work with their team to establish a set of safety rules for their class. Recognizing the need to ensure the children's safety through a consistent approach by all members of the team, they identify potential dangers in their own environment, both indoors and out, and suggest ways of avoiding these dangers. In some cases, parents are asked to say what they think might be dangerous and how they would like to see staff deal with this. The results of this process are written up as a set of safety rules, to be given to all staff working in the nursery and displayed in prominent places for the benefit of relief staff and parents.

For example, in one school the toilet doors, which were saloon bar style, were difficult for children to manage and, in anticipation of possible problems, a rule was written indicating that all new children needed to be shown how to use the toilet doors safely. A rule for the outside area of an inner-city class made it clear that the playground should be checked daily for rubbish, small pieces of glass and so on by the member of staff setting out the outdoor equipment.

To most nursery teams, keeping the nursery environment and the children safe and clean is something they do without too much thought as a matter of course. For this reason they do not always talk about it. However, discussions with parents reveal that many of them are greatly reassured to hear more from the staff about safety. It is quite natural for parents to worry about the safety of their very precious child and it is up to nursery teachers to demonstrate that they have done everything possible to ensure this safety.

Safety and outings

Sometimes children are taken out of the school grounds. Parents are asked to sign a consent form giving their agreement to this. Outings into the local community are a regular and very important part of the nursery curriculum and parents will want to know that their child is safe. They have the right to ask that their child is not included in outings if they are not satisfied with arrangements. Most local authorities will give advice on the ratio of adults to children allowed for outings, but common sense usually leads nursery teachers to ensure that all children are held by the hand when going on outings in busy streets. This obviously requires parents to be involved, and the teacher has to ensure they are aware of their responsibility for ensuring children's safety, as well as for helping the children to gain educationally from the outing. Sharing responsibility in this way helps parents to understand how seriously the nursery teacher takes the children's safety, and gives reassurance to parents in the process.

Coping with accidents

Parents who have gained confidence in the nursery staff through involvement in policy-making and practice will be much more able to cope with the inevitable accidents which happen to children. Three- to five-year-olds are still learning how to control their bodies, and it is inevitable that they will sometimes bump into things, trip or fall over as they practise and refine their physical skills. Most accidents are of the scraped knee variety but occasionally a more serious injury is sustained. Rachel, while walking along a relatively low and very stable wooden box set up in a large space in the carpeted area of the classroom, was suddenly distracted by something across the room, and walked off the edge of the box before the teacher could do anything about it. She fell awkwardly on her arm, which fractured. In this kind of situation teachers need to ensure that parents are given clear, calm and accurate information about what happened. This is never easy since no parent copes well with seeing their child hurt in any way, and teachers inevitably feel responsible even when it would have been unrealistic to expect that the accident could have been prevented.

Coping with aggression

Even more difficult to cope with are the injuries inflicted by one child on another. As part of learning to be a member of a group, young children have to learn to cope with the frustrations involved in sharing with others and with taking turns. Often their attempts to get a turn or to stop someone from taking what they want are unsophisticated and even brutal. They still have to learn how to sort out their problems verbally, and the more limited their language skills, the more they will resort to other methods of communication. Biting, kicking, scratching and hair pulling are sometimes the only methods they can think of to get what they want. When explaining to the parents of the victim or the aggressor, it is important that the nursery teacher explains the reasons for this behaviour. It is easy for a young child to be labelled a bully, and even for that child and their family to be made scapegoats. This situation may reinforce the child's aggressive behaviour. It is very important that this does not happen, since all children have to be given the chance to outgrow what is essentially immature behaviour. Just because a child bites at 3 does not mean he will be a biter at 10. He may well be though, if he thinks that we expect him to be.

Coping with risk

In addition to her responsibility to create a safe physical environment for the children, the teacher has to foster the kind of ethos that will encourage all members of the school community to accept that growing up involves taking risks and sometimes getting hurt or hurting someone else. She has to help all adults to put this risk taking into perspective and deal with it constructively. Children cannot be totally shielded from the risks, but they can be helped to learn from the consequences of their actions. The child who was bitten because he snatched a toy from another child can be taught to ask for a turn, and the biter can be encouraged to talk about her anger or tell an adult what has happened. Similarly, the child who fell because her attention wavered could be helped to learn that she needs to concentrate when climbing. Through sharing these strategies with parents a more consistent approach to nursery discipline can be achieved.

Dealing with conflict between parents and staff

Conflict can arise when parents and teachers disagree about the most appropriate strategy. Some parents encourage their child to hit back if they have been hurt, for fear that any other strategy will lead to the child being bullied. This is clearly not a response which nursery staff would wish to encourage, yet neither do they want to seem to be dictating to parents how they bring up their child. This kind of conflict is often regarded as one of the most difficult aspects of their relationship with parents.

It can usually be resolved through a discussion of responsibilities. The teacher is ultimately responsible for what happens in her class. She will listen to the views of others and will take these views into account but, ultimately, she has to decide what is in the best interests of the group as a whole. Parents have a similar responsibility to decide what happens in their home.

Generally, parents are quite happy to accept school rules if:

- They know them, understand them and were asked for their point of view.
- They trust the teacher and other staff to ensure that these rules are fairly and consistently enforced.
- They are confident that their children will be protected (through the enforcement of the rules) from bullying, and will develop strategies for standing up to those who seek to dominate them.
- They are able to see that their children's behaviour is maturing.
- They witness a calm, caring atmosphere when they come into the nursery class.

It can be seen that in order to ensure children's physical security and safety, their feelings also need to be taken into account. Many dangerous situations develop from frustration, anger or from feelings of inadequacy. The creation of a physically safe environment depends at least to some extent on the teacher's ability to help children understand and cope with their feelings.

The Need for Emotional Security

Earlier in this chapter we saw the link between intellectual development and emotional well-being. Adults sometimes forget this link, and yet if you ask them to recall memories of their own early school experiences they will relate a whole series of horror stories and fears – often connected with toilets, being forced to eat food or being made to look foolish by an adult, which undoubtedly had an effect on their ability to learn, as well as on their feelings about themselves. Similarly, many adults walking into a new situation will admit to feeling apprehensive and to wondering whether they will be able to do what is expected of them, and whether there will be anyone they know present. They acknowledge that their confidence would be shattered if they were suddenly asked to do something unexpected such as give a talk to a large group of people. Most adults also admit they would feel very insecure within a situation where no one understood their language.

Emotional security seems to stem from:

1. Knowing what to expect from a situation (it helps if the situation is one which has been successfully coped with before).
2. Being well prepared for the new experience, and being motivated to take part in it.
3. Knowing someone in the new setting.
4. Being able to understand what is going on.
5. Being allowed to take things at our own pace and not being singled out too early.
6. Being encouraged by others and not made to look foolish.

Often adults are inhibited from trying something new because of previous negative experiences. For example, many adults, particularly women, fear being asked to take part in a technological activity because they were made to feel incapable of such tasks in the past.

The main difference between adults and very young children is that adults have a wealth of previous experience to draw on, which either helps them to cope with new situations and expectations or inhibits them. The younger the child, the less life experience he or she has. Much of what happens to him or her is happening for the first time. When children encounter a new situation they generally have no negative feelings about it – unless adults or older children have transferred their worries to them or unless they are tired or ill. They are open to the new experience and their feelings about it will develop positively or negatively depending on how they are treated.

Consider the 3-year-old boy (or girl) starting at nursery class. Often this is the child's first separation from his family, which has provided the setting for his development so far. Within this familiar setting he has been known and valued as an individual, his identity, language and culture have been developed and reinforced, and he has learnt the rules for functioning. By the time he is old enough for nursery class he has already built up a view of himself and the world – his own world. Most children are confident and competent operators within their home setting (Wells, 1986).

On starting nursery class he is expected to move from this relatively secure environment into one where there are many more children than he has seen before, with whom he has to share equipment and adult time; where he has to relate to unfamiliar adults who do not always understand his approaches and who may not even speak his language; where he does not know what is expected and keeps getting things wrong; and where there are adults who do not always seem to understand or value the things he has learnt at home. It is hardly surprising that many children find the transition from home to nursery class difficult at least to some extent (Blatchford, Battle and Mays, 1982). The early weeks are very important. What happens to the child during this time and afterwards will determine whether he or she is able to operate just as confidently in his or her new environment or whether his or her self-esteem will be damaged.

Young children need support to enable them to adjust to temporary separation from their family. They need to feel that they are a valuable competent member of the new social group, and they need to develop positive attitudes towards the range of new experiences they will encounter at nursery class. Above all they need to be helped to retain the self-confidence and self-respect they have already gained.

Encouraging Emotional Security

It is the teacher's job to ensure that she and her team build on the work of the family and take steps to ensure that the child is valued as an individual at school as well as at home. This sounds a considerably easier task than it actually is. Children enter nursery class from a variety of backgrounds and respond to it in many different ways. The teacher may not always know about worries the child may have, since these worries sometimes surface at home rather than at school. Caroline (3 years) told her mother that she never used the toilet at nursery because the toilet paper was 'scratchy on my bottom'. She had become quite anxious about needing to go to the toilet and not wanting to go. The problem was resolved when her mother talked to the nursery staff, and the teacher was able to use this child's anxiety to argue for softer toilet paper for the nursery children.

If she is to help individual children to adjust to the different demands of the nursery school without losing their individual identity, the teacher has to ensure that the ethos and learning environment she creates are responsive. This means they must be flexible enough to cater for the entire range of needs.

Sharing information

If the teacher wants to know about children she must talk to parents. Parents can provide a wealth of knowledge about their children and are generally very keen to share this with the nursery staff. Through talking with parents, teachers gain the insights they need to make the transition from home to nursery class as smooth as possible. Getting to know the child and planning for admission to nursery class requires parents and teachers to engage in 'an equal partnership in which both learn from each other' (Hazareesingh, Simms and Anderson, 1989). Teachers can learn from parents how to respond to a particular child, and parents can learn from teachers how they can contribute to their child's security at school.

In spite of lack of time, teachers regard this sharing as vital, and have built a variety of opportunities for this kind of communication into their practice. Some nursery classes and schools have toddler groups attached, which teachers and nursery nurses visit regularly, so links are built up from a very early age. Visits to the nursery class prior to a child's admission are also arranged. During these visits the child becomes familiar with the new situation, and the parents and teacher have the chance to share information and concerns. Some teachers offer to visit families at home (always respecting the parents' right to say 'no thank you'!), to give parents the chance to talk in more detail about their child and to ask any questions about nursery education, and also to demonstrate to the child the close link which is developing between his or her parents and the teacher. Sometimes teachers will share these responsibilities with nursery nurses. In this case, the member of staff who has visited the family will usually maintain the link during the settling in period. Whichever member of staff is involved in initial communications, the teacher is responsible for ensuring consistency of approach, and all members of the basic team (see Chapter 1) need to have information about the child.

Each nursery team, in consultation with parents, who often have strong views about what they wish to tell the nursery staff, will decide what information would be useful to them and how they will record it. This aspect of recordkeeping is explored in more detail in Chapter 4.

Establishing a welcoming environment for parents

How willing parents are to share what they know about their children will depend on the kind of environment the nursery teacher offers them.

Parents need to feel that their presence is welcomed. Many of them have memories of school which make them feel apprehensive about entering educational establishments and approaching teachers.

Influenced by research evidence (in particular Smith, 1980, and Tizard, Mortimore and Burchell, 1981) teachers have realized that collaboration with parents is a vital part of their role as carer and educator of young children, and have worked very hard to create the kind of relaxed, informal atmosphere within their classes which will encourage all parents to participate. They have recognized that they:

- Must organize their time so that they are free at the beginning and end of a session to welcome and talk informally with parents – particularly those who are least confident in the school situation.
- Need to be flexible so that all parents have the chance to contribute to their child's education. This requires them to make opportunities to talk with working parents, and seek the support of translators and interpreters to ensure that all parents, whatever language they speak, are given equal access to information and equal opportunities to share their knowledge of their child. Many teachers have had to acquire the skill of communicating via an interpreter.
- Must demonstrate their respect for parents' knowledge by asking for their views and by listening to what they say. Just as they must have high expectations of all children, so they must believe that all parents are capable of contributing valid views.
- Need to help parents to gain the confidence to contribute within the school situation. This confidence will generally be the result of the teacher's work in all the above areas. It is also necessary for teachers to make their expectations clear to parents. For example, if a home visit is proposed by the teacher she must ensure parents understand the purpose of such a proposal, as well as respecting the parent's right to reject the suggestion. Tizard, Mortimore and Burchell (1981) found that parents welcome this kind of involvement if they have a clear understanding of the purpose.

Establishing an atmosphere of trust and equality takes time. Teachers recognize that, if parents have confidence in, and understand, the educational aims of the staff, the children will benefit. An investment of time before the child starts nursery generally results in a much smoother transition from home to school because parents are better equipped to support staff before and during the settling in period.

Preparing children for admission

Both parents and staff want children to enjoy school, and increasingly they see the need to work together to prepare children in advance for new experiences. Through pre-admission visits and home visits parents and children begin to know what to expect from school, and the staff get to know the family.

Sometimes teachers will make photo books of life in the nursery class for parents and children to borrow and discuss at home. These books include photos with captions of all areas of the nursery including toilets, and show what happens at all times of the day, from hanging up coats on personal pegs, to going home at the end of the session. Through discussing the book with their parents, children gain a much clearer view of what will happen and some possible anxieties are minimized. For example, many children are concerned that they will be left overnight, and are greatly relieved when their parents emphasize the section of the book which deals with going home time.

This kind of preparation depends on teachers and parents working together in the interests of the child. Together they can anticipate any aspects of school life the child may find difficult and can plan to help the child cope with these.

Settling children into the class

The effort parents and staff have made in advance always pays off once children are admitted. Parents and children know what to expect and teachers and nursery nurses know enough about each child to ensure that they can respond to individual needs.

Admissions should be organized on a staggered basis so that the person who has made the closest contact with the family is available to greet them and give time to them on their first day. Earlier in this chapter, the need to know someone in the new setting was stressed. Although the family will know at least one member of the nursery staff, young children, who often find it difficult to express their needs verbally, also need the support of their parents or regular caregiver during the settling in period. This needs to be explained to parents well in advance so that they understand why their child needs them and can make appropriate arrangements. How long this support will be needed depends on the child and is generally negotiated between the parent and the teacher. During the first few days the assigned staff member will make sure that she gives personal time to the child and parent, if necessary with the help of someone who speaks the family's language, so that both develop confidence in the relationship.

The nursery class offers a bewildering array of tempting opportunities for the child. Teachers work with their team to ensure that during their first few days each child finds something familiar within the class which he or she can relate to as well as new and stimulating opportunities. Teachers also have to create an environment which reflects the society the children live in and which questions stereotypical ideas about the roles which men and women, and black and white people, can take. This challenge is as important for children living in predominantly white areas, as it is for those living in multicultural areas. The environment teachers create gives important messages to children and parents about what they value. Teachers have to give thought to the equipment and experiences they offer, the displays they set up and the way they spend their time.

Only if they have given this careful consideration will they be sure that children will find the familiar resources they need for security and self-esteem within the new situation. Anyone who has seen the expression of joy and excitement on the face of the child who has spotted the book, poster or dressing up outfit which reminds him or her of home, will understand the importance of resources to the child's emotional security. It is as important for the child who lives in a high rise flat to find books and pictures of tower blocks, as it is for the Chinese child to find books and pictures of Chinese people in Britain. If children are aware that their background is acknowledged and valued they will be well equipped to acknowledge and value backgrounds of other children.

Teachers are powerful role models for the children and have a responsibility to help children develop positive attitudes to themselves and to others. For example, if the staff are seen to cook, and to encourage parents to cook, a wide variety of foods, and then to eat these foods enthusiastically, children are more likely to want to try them and less likely to reject anything unfamiliar by calling it 'yukky'.

Small children are greatly reassured if they find equipment in school, such as Lego or a favourite book, which they have already used at home. Using the knowledge which parents have shared with them, nursery staff can help children find familiar resources in the class.

To cater for the wide range of needs and interests the teacher has to organize her class so that equipment is easily accessible to the children. It should be stored and labelled (perhaps with pictures) so that children can see what is available, get it out and then put it away when they have finished using it. Parents are often asked to help their child get used to making choices, using equipment safely, and taking responsibility for their actions in this way. Right from the start children are encouraged to feel powerful members of the class, secure in the knowledge that they have some choice and control over what happens to them within the framework of a set of consistent safety rules.

Once a child is able to use all parts of the nursery class confidently and feels at ease with at least one member of staff, parents can feel quite happy about leaving him or her. Usually, teachers will advise parents to leave their child for just a short period at first, in case the child should become distressed, building up the time gradually until the child stays contentedly for the full session. Many teachers and parents know that this kind of gradual separation is very important for young children if they are not to suffer the kind of distress described by those who have researched the experience of some 4-year-olds in reception classes. Bennett and Kell (1989) describe graphically how deeply distressed young children can become when they are inadequately prepared for new experiences – there is after all little worse than fear of the unknown.

Maintaining emotional security

So far we have focused on how the nursery teacher supports the child emotionally during the potentially traumatic transition from home to school. A positive start is vital but the teacher's concern for children's feelings does not stop there. Throughout the remainder of each child's time in nursery education she has to continue to foster emotional development. She has to:

- Help each child express and cope with his or her feelings in constructive rather than destructive, assertive rather than aggressive or passive, ways. This will be examined in detail in Chapter 3.
- Make sure that each child's achievements are recognized and encouraged so that all children retain positive attitudes towards learning. This requires her to focus on what children can do and build on these skills rather than concentrating on the things the child has not yet achieved. Through focusing her attention in this way and acknowledging each child's individual effort and progress, she encourages a sense of achievement rather than a sense of failure.
- Provide opportunities for children to come to terms with their fears and anxieties through their play experiences. For example, Jane's baby sister was seriously ill and had been taken into hospital. Jane's mother (a lone parent) was temporarily living in at the hospital and Jane was being cared for by her grandmother. Jane's teacher noticed her pushing a baby

doll through the nursery class in a pushchair. As Jane passed she told her teacher 'She's really, really sick in her tummy. I got to take her to the hopital.' The teacher played the part of a concerned friend asking about the baby's illness and about who would be looking after the baby's brothers and sisters while Jane took the baby to hospital. In this way, she helped Jane to express some of her fears about what was happening in her family. At the end of the session she told Jane's grandmother what had happened so that she too could offer Jane some support.

- Help children to develop the skills they need to stand up for themselves and challenge aggressive, racist or sexist approaches. In recent years, this work has developed to help children protect themselves from abuse by adults (Pen Green Family Centre, 1990). How teachers help children develop these skills will be explored in Chapter 3.
- Notice changes in behaviour which may signify worries or insecurity. One of the times when behavioural changes are most likely to occur is after the birth of a sibling. Parents and staff can work together to help the child respond positively to the new arrival.

Nursery teachers need to create an atmosphere of respect and trust with children just as they have to with parents. Children will only open up discussions with adults who have demonstrated their willingness to listen, and to respond to what children have to say. The most effective nursery settings are those where children have been encouraged to talk openly about their feelings even if that involves being critical of an adult. Tom (4 years 2 months) was very angry with his teacher one afternoon because, after reminding him several times that it was dangerous to push others when they were climbing, she had asked him to move away from the climbing frame. He was clearly upset that his testing of the rules had led to him being asked to leave an area he enjoyed playing in. In frustration (with himself as much as anyone), he turned on his teacher and said 'I think it's time you found another school!' Rather than punishing him further for what could have been seen as rudeness, the teacher spent some time with him helping him to understand the frustration he was feeling, and helping him to see how his need to test the rules to the limit had led to disappointment. With this approach he was less likely to become resentful and more likely to understand why some rules are non-negotiable.

To approach her work in this way the teacher needs to be able to share power with children and their parents. She cannot adopt the role of all-knowing professional. Power sharing is only possible if teachers feel secure in and confident of their own skills. Lack of confidence often leads to defensiveness, and an unwillingness to share with others for fear of being made to seem inadequate. Well-trained nursery teachers are confident in their skills, and aware of their own strengths and weaknesses, but less well trained teachers of young children admit that they worry about working with parents because they are afraid of being challenged. This highlights once again the need for trainers on initial and in-service courses to ensure that teachers develop confidence in their knowledge of child development and are able to articulate clearly their approach to others. The self-esteem and confidence of teachers directly affects their ability to offer an environment which enhances the self-esteem and confidence of children and their parents.

In order to be able to identify and meet children's individual needs, nursery teachers need to make time to observe children to find out what they are feeling, and how they are responding to nursery life. In Chapters 4 and 5 this will be explained further. Helping children to identify and express their feelings is closely linked to the work the nursery teacher has to do to enable children to cope with a new social situation. It is this aspect of a child's development which is explored in the next chapter.

Some Points for Discussion

Equality of Opportunity

Awareness raising

In which ways have you made (could you make) yourself and your team aware of:

- Inequalities in society?
- Inequalities within the education system?
- Attitudes (your own included) which may lead to discrimination against some children and families?
- Practices within your own school and class which may reinforce existing inequalities? Think about admissions policies, your own involvement – and non-involvement – with parents and children, and in activities, etc.
- The children who dominate and those who are dominated by others? Including the children who are given most/least adult attention.
- The children who are confident and assertive and those who are aggressive or timid?
- Discriminatory language used or remarks made by staff, children, parents or visitors?
- The objective views of visitors to your class?

Taking positive action

Being aware of inequality, the reasons for it, and the ways in which it is consciously and unconsciously reinforced is essential if the need for positive action is to be understood. The next step is to work towards a set of beliefs:

- What kinds of opportunities do you believe all children, parents and staff should be offered in the nursery class? Write down your beliefs in the form of an equal opportunities statement.
- Taking each belief in turn ask yourselves: how will we make sure that each of these beliefs is put into practice? For example, if we believe that all children should have access to a broad, balanced curriculum how will we encourage this? The results of this discussion will form an equal opportunities policy or action plan.

Monitoring equal opportunities policies

Unless your work is regularly evaluated it is impossible to be sure that what you intended is being put into practice consistently. How will you check that your policy is being put into practice by all team members?

Physical and Emotional Security

Health and safety

- What steps have you taken to ensure that the nursery environment is clean and safe? Does everyone understand their responsibilities? Do parents know how you make sure the nursery is kept clean and how you ensure their child's safety?
- What are the rules in your class? How do you ensure that staff, children and parents know them and understand the reasons for them? How do you reinforce these rules on a daily basis?
- Are there any areas of conflict between staff and parents? What are the reasons for this conflict? Is there any way of resolving it?

Emotional security

- What opportunities do you provide for all parents to tell you about their child, and to hear from you about the nursery class?
- Think of yourself spending time in a place which is not your home – what does it take for you to feel welcome?

- How do you make all parents feel welcome in your class? (Think about dads, parents with babies and toddlers, parents who speak little or no English, etc.)
- How could you find out whether all parents feel welcome?

Managing the Transition from Home to Nursery

- What kind of admissions policy would enable you to get to know and respond to each child as an individual?
- Which aspects of life in your class are likely to be stressful for a young child starting school for the first time? (Think about toilets, noise, numbers of other children, unknown adults, care of personal possessions, etc.)
- What steps could you take to minimize stress? How do you ensure that the child adjusts gradually, i.e. without shock, to the new environment and to new expectations? Are your settling in procedures flexible enough to cater for individual needs?
- How could you involve each child's parents or carer in supporting the child during the transition from home to nursery class? What opportunities do you provide for parents and children to discuss their concerns with you during the settling in period? How do you encourage both children and parents to discuss their feelings openly with you throughout their time in the nursery class?

Ongoing Emotional Support

- During their time in the nursery class children will be encouraged to take part in a variety of new experiences (e.g. staying for lunch) and new challenges – how do you help children to approach these with confidence rather than fear?
- How do you work with infant teacher colleagues to ensure that transfer from the nursery class to the reception class is also as stress-free as possible?

3
HELPING CHILDREN TO 'BRANCH OUT'

The Need to Develop Social Strategies

The previous chapter gave some of the demands which transition from the family to a wider social group make on the young child. Admission to a nursery class requires children to extend the range of interpersonal strategies they have already built up at home. The skill involved in supporting this development is often underestimated. Teachers of older children may not realize the demands which are made on nursery teachers as they help children to develop a range of behaviours appropriate to the school setting – and yet infant teachers often remark 'You can always tell the children who have been to nursery class, they know how to behave!'

Teaching Style and the Development of Social Strategies

There is often confusion about the type of help nursery teachers give to encourage social development. Young children are physically small and usually eager to please their teachers (Katz and Chard, 1989), and it is therefore relatively easy to control them and make them conform within an adult directed environment. Effective nursery teachers do not take the easy way out, however. They are aware that domination by adults may lead to some children modelling this controlling behaviour, and dominating or bullying other children. This would obviously not be a desirable outcome in view of the already stated aim to offer all children equality of opportunity. Experienced teachers comment that the greatest overall change in their practice over the last ten years or so has been in relation to their approach to the children.

Inspired by the research of Wood, McMahon and Cranstoun (1980) they realized too much of their time was being spent managing and controlling children, and not enough was being spent on observing, listening to and conversing with them. The importance of the development of social competence in the early years for later life has also been emphasized in research (Asher, Renshaw and Hymel, 1982), and the need for the teacher to intervene 'in the course of interactions with peers' (Katz and Chard, 1989, p. 26), rather than through formal instruction, is stressed. As a result of this research the controlling approach, which encourages dependence on others, has come to be seen as inappropriate.

Teachers have become aware that, if they hope all children will become self-motivated, competent operators in and out of the school situation, their teaching style needs to be of the kind which empowers and enourages autonomous behaviour. Much time is currently being spent on in-service courses discussing what 'autonomy' means and how we would know an autonomous individual if we saw one. As Blenkin and Kelly (1987, p. 9) make clear, autonomy is not an end-state 'towards which we must strive' but a procedural principle 'by which it is suggested we should live, and, as teachers, help our pupils to live'. In order to encourage children to live autonomously teachers need to inspire them to:

- believe that they have the power and ability to control their own lives,
- make informed choices,
- get involved and enjoy challenges,
- plan their own time,
- use others as a resource,
- take responsibility for their own actions and choices,
- respect others (living autonomously does not mean pursuing one's own interests without regard for others).

These are complex abilities which many adults have not been encouraged to develop themselves. There is increasing evidence that if children begin to develop these abilities in the early years, they will be well equipped to gain maximum benefit from early education and also to cope with the challenges of later life: 'the early education experience may change children from passive to active learners who begin to take the initiative in seeking information, help, and interaction with others' (Lazar and Darlington, 1982, p. 63).

Supporting Social Development

Before considering the best way of helping children's social development it is necessary to clarify the new demands the class will make on them. Nursery education requires young children to develop as individuals and also as a member of their peer group. These two aspects of development are interrelated: the growth of self-awareness is closely linked with the 'sense of others, their needs and their sometimes conflicting impingement on our own personal space and identity' (Blenkin and Whitehead, 1987, p. 40).

In order to be able to interact harmoniously within a group, young children need to feel confident and secure about their own rights and position. As we saw above they need to feel valued, respected and cared about so they can value, respect and care about others.

Life within the nursery class requires children to share equipment and adult time, make choices and compromises, take turns, take responsibility for their own actions and generally to take into account the needs of others in the group. Gradually, they have to develop a range of skills relevant to this new social situation.

Learning to share equipment and take turns

The nursery class environment, because it has been set up to serve the needs and interests of young children, offers a treasure trove of delights for the 3-year-old on his or her first visit. Children's response to this paradise varies. Some children want it all at once and race from area to area sampling the activities and equipment on offer. Others seek out one piece of equipment which attracts their attention – often something they are already familiar with – and stay with this to begin with. Others appear totally bewildered and refuse to leave their carer's side.

In their early days at nursery, children have to learn that they have the right to choose from and use all the equipment, but that it does not belong to them exclusively – they cannot take it home, for example. Part of this learning process involves discovering that some pieces of equipment, such as construction kits or the climbing frame, are to be used simultaneously by more than one child, while others, such as headphones or a sand spade, are to be used by one child at a time.

How much experience of sharing and turntaking each child will have gained before starting nursery class will depend on family size and attendance at pre-school groups, but most children will never before have been expected to share so much with so many. Merely putting children together will not in itself ensure that they learn this social skill. They need the continuous support and encouragement of adults. It is a major part of the role of the teacher to help all children to operate confidently within the nursery situation, to select and make use of the equipment they need while respecting the needs of others.

Helping children to share equipment and take turns

The teacher's first responsibility is to ensure that her class is adequately resourced. Resources should be available as much of the time as possible and there should be enough of them to encourage imaginative use. It is best to have a large quantity of one construction set, which several children can use productively at once, than small quantities of several different sets none of which offer even one child the chance to build in depth.

Similarly, teachers have realized that making as much equipment as possible available for children to choose from every day is the best way of encouraging sharing and turntaking. In classes where staff limit the activities on offer, or the time available to use equipment, there is often an air of desperation about the children, who know that if they do not get a turn now, they may not get one at all before the equipment is put away. If they know that what is available today will still be available tomorrow they are certain to be more relaxed about their involvement.

Children are less likely to hoard all the equipment for themselves if they can see that there will be enough for them even if others use some, or that they will have plenty of time to have a turn after other children have finished. Sometimes teachers help children to understand that there is enough for everyone by offering them a similar, alternative piece of equipment. This is a useful interim strategy as children are learning but, ultimately, teachers aim to help children consider the interests of others as well as their own. They have to judge when each child is able to begin to identify and empathize with others in this way. Communication skills are the determining factor here, since children need to be able to make sense of the teacher's verbal explanations.

The ways in which young children express their frustration when others take their toy, or will not give them a turn, have already been discussed. It is the teacher's job to help children express these frustrations in words rather than aggressive deeds, and to help them to consider the points of view of others as well as their own. She does this by talking each situation through with the children involved and helping them to reach a solution to their problem which is appropriate to their level of understanding.

Samantha and Wahida (two 3-year-olds) were playing alongside each other at the sand tray. Samantha was filling a bucket using a spade, while Wahida was piling sand up in the corner of the tray with her hands. Wahida suddenly seemed to decide she needed a spade to pat down the top of her pile of sand and grabbed the spade which Samantha was using. A brief 'tug of war' ensued and both girls screamed loudly. The teacher who had been observing the incident intervened at this point. She talked quietly to the two girls explaining to Wahida that Samantha was using the spade to fill her bucket and that if she wanted a spade she could choose one from the trolley next to the sand tray. She proceeded to help Wahida make her choice and the play continued smoothly.

In this particular case, the girls were both new to nursery class and had not yet got used to selecting equipment from the range available. The teacher's main priority was therefore to draw their attention to the choices available to them. However, she also began the process of signalling to them the need to respect the activities of others.

As children gain in experience and maturity, teachers use such situations to model ways for the children to negotiate with each other. Caroline and Natalie were both well settled at nursery school and often played together. One morning Caroline had been playing on the tricycle for some time and Natalie wanted a turn, so she tried to push Caroline off the tricycle. The nursery teacher helped her to find an alternative way of receiving a turn by working through a negotiation process with her. She encouraged Natalie to say 'Can I have a turn?' and when Caroline said 'I haven't finished yet', helped her to negotiate a timescale which would give Caroline one more circuit of the playground before it was her turn. The teacher stayed with the girls long enough to ensure that Natalie got her turn, and also observed the girls over the next few weeks and supported Natalie's subsequent attempts to negotiate. This ongoing support is important if children are not to get discouraged. They need to be able to see that alternatives to aggression can be just as effective.

Of course, just because a child asks nicely they may not get a turn there and then. Children also have to learn when it is inappropriate to expect another child to give up something they are using – when they have just begun to use it, or when the piece of equipment is central to a lengthy project, for example. This is where children on both sides of the situation can be helped to reason with each other and begin to understand how it feels to be the other person. So, when Natalie several days later approached another child who had just got on the bike and asked for a turn, it was necessary for the teacher to help her to see how she would feel if she had just started to use the bike and someone wanted her to get off.

Naturally, children will try to test out how far they can go in this situation. It is not long before a child asked to give up the tricycle after two more circuits realizes that she can prolong her ride by cycling very slowly – causing great frustration to the child waiting for a turn and testing the patience of the adult. A sensitive teacher can use these situations to help children become more self-aware and also more aware of the feelings of others – for example by saying to the bike rider 'I know you would like to ride the tricycle for much longer and don't want to give it up, but . . . hasn't had a turn at all, and you know how unhappy you would be if you hadn't had a turn.'

By talking through disputes and emphasizing feelings in this way, teachers offer some verbal strategies for children to employ and help them to empathize with others. Before long children are able to invent their own strategies for other situations – it was not long before Natalie was overheard suggesting to another child that she should be given a turn with a sand wheel 'when you've tipped that bucket in'. Older children will also delight in helping younger ones to develop the skills they have already learnt. Nothing is more rewarding for the teacher than to overhear an experienced child kindly explaining to a newcomer why he or she should allow another child to share or have a turn. This is why nursery classes need 4-year-olds. Nursery teachers who lose their 4-year-olds to reception classes comment that the remaining 3-year-olds are at a disadvantage when they have no slightly older role models. In the same way, nursery classes where predominantly 4-year-olds are admitted (due to pressure on places) do not offer the children a chance to care about and take responsibility for the younger ones. A balance of 3- and 4-year-olds is essential.

Supporting children's development in this way is an extremely time-consuming process, and requires both vigilance and patience on the part of the teacher and her team. It is no good beginning the process one day and forgetting all about it the next, since only when consistent efforts are made will children really be able to feel confident that aggression does not pay. Above all adults must be seen to be fair. Even the very youngest children are quick to notice unjust treatment.

Encouraging assertive behaviour

Research has confirmed what many staff already know about the domination of certain areas of experience by particular children (see section on equal opportunities in Chapter 2). Teachers have to ensure that some children are not excluded from taking part in the full range of experiences. How they ensure a broad curriculum for each child is explored in Chapters 4 and 5, but an important aspect of their role is to help children stand up for themselves in the face of intimidation or bullying by others who want to exclude them.

This is a relatively new focus for the nursery teacher emanating from their concern to give all children greater control over their own lives. Teachers have realized that both passive and aggressive children are at a disadvantage and that aggression thrives on passivity in the nursery classroom and in the wider society. With the increased awareness of child abuse they also know that children need to be aware that adults are not always to be trusted. These are difficult issues to deal with with such young and vulnerable children and there is no easy approach.

Existing practice indicates that assertive behaviour is most likely to be encouraged in a situation:

- Where aggressive behaviour is not rewarded (even unintentionally).
- Where adults treat children as people with equal rights who are entitled to put forward their opinion and challenge adults if necessary.
- Where passive or withdrawn children are actively encouraged to develop in confidence – this requires teachers to take time away from the more demanding children in their group, and concentrate on the needs of the least demanding individuals, and is easier said than done.
- In an informal environment where adults including parents see their role as empowering rather than controlling children – offering children strategies and reasons rather than telling children what to do and expecting unquestioning obedience.

Some staff have begun to formalize this work, even writing about their experiences in one instance (Pen Green Family Centre, 1990).

Teachers need regularly to assess the progress of the children in their class to see how far all children are being helped. This is discussed in more detail in Chapter 4.

Interacting with adults

In order to develop in the ways suggested above, children need to be able to approach adults and use them as a resource. This is why the initial contact with nursery staff is so important. During their first few days at nursery class, priority is given to ensuring that each child and his or her parent are given individual attention. In this way the child is made to feel valued and begins to gain confidence in the new adults.

Some children find sharing their 'special adult' (teacher) with other children very difficult, especially if they have been used to a close one-to-one relationship with an adult at home. Paul had been brought up on a farm on the fringes of a northern new town. He was the only child of older parents and had spent most of his pre-school life in the company of adults. He found it difficult to relate to the other children in his class who all lived in the new town and did not share his enthusiasm for farming. Consequently, he stayed very close to his teacher's side during his first few weeks at school and needed a lot of support to develop relationships with his peers.

Some children relate happily to the other children but are less confident about approaching a teacher or nursery nurse. Claudia, an articulate child with her peers and mother, refused to speak to any member of the staff. The staff could only guess at why this was the case and had to wait patiently for her to feel comfortable with them. They were careful not to pressurize her by asking questions, but talked to her in the course of activities. One day, nearly three terms after she had been admitted, Claudia started to talk to her teacher as if she had been doing so all her life and from that day onward there was no stopping her. In this case patience was rewarded. If the staff had put pressure on Claudia in any way it is unlikely that this outcome would have been achieved.

As well as learning to share equipment children also have to learn to share adult time. They have the right to expect that they will receive some individual attention, but also have to learn that others have the same right. Some of the disruptive or withdrawn behaviour which children exhibit in nursery classes is their attempt to gain attention from the adults.

Helping all children to establish positive relationships with adults

Nursery teachers are well aware that it is easy to make the mistake of responding to children on demand, enabling some children (the more dominant ones) to take up most of their time at the expense of the quieter, less demanding children. It is not easy to ensure that attention is given equally to children, but it is the teacher's responsibility to ensure that she monitors how she and her team spend their time – where, with whom and for what purpose.

They need to create an environment where staff have time to listen to children's concerns and where children are encouraged to use adults as a resource. This kind of environment depends on adults being free from the management and control of resources and activities, and on children being encouraged to develop their own interests using readily available and accessible materials.

Children gain powerful messages from adult behaviour and very quickly learn whether or not it is worth trying to tell an adult something. They ar not likely to engage in conversation with an adult who is constantly 'busy'. On the other hand, they are very likely to approach again the adult who expresses an interest in their activities, and who shares her experiences with them (Wood, McMahon and Cranstoun, 1980). It is this kind of equality in interaction that teachers aim for because it offers children a secure base from which to develop the confidence to tell, ask, question, and discuss. The development of communication skills will be discussed in more depth later in this chapter.

Learning to care and take responsibility

Already in this chapter we have seen how children starting nursery education gradually need to learn to accept the responsibilities involved in being part of a larger social group. Teachers have to help them to understand that they are responsible for their own actions and choices, and that they share a collective responsibility for the environment and equipment. As they get older, the children are helped to empathize with and take some responsibility for younger members of the group.

Children will only learn to take responsibility if they are given responsibility. Teachers, who with their teams, have organized their classes to encourage greater autonomy and independence, have often been surprised by the children's achievements. They have realized that children do live up to adult expectations. They have also learnt that patient support from adults is crucial. Similarly, parents are often surprised to discover that their child can cope with self-help tasks, such as going to the toilet, dressing and undressing, and eating with a knife and fork in the nursery situation.

Taking responsibility for own actions and choices

Whichever social group we belong to, certain individual and collective responsibilities are inevitable. Within the nursery class children are encouraged to make choices but quickly learn that they are responsible for the outcomes of these choices. Above all they are helped to understand that the choices they make should not limit the options of other children – that whatever they do they must always consider the other members of the group. Earlier in this chapter we saw how teachers help young children to understand that others have an equal right to use equipment and that turns have to be taken. Children also have to learn that they share responsibility for maintaining a clean, orderly environment.

For example, when they have finished using a piece of equipment they are expected to put it back ready for the next child. If they choose to work with art materials they are expected to clean up the area when they have finished, and if they play with sand they need to sweep up any spills. These responsibilities are seen by teachers as a central part of nursery life and the beginning of each new term is spent reminding the older children of expectations they may have forgotten about during the school holidays, and supporting the new children as they adjust to the new social situation.

Young children generally enjoy taking on what they often see as adult responsibilities. At home they enjoy helping their parents with household chores, such as washing up or dusting. Teachers and nursery nurses who see tidying up and cleaning up as powerful learning experiences, are able to build on this natural enthusiasm and turn chores into fun for adults and children alike.

The learning environment has to be resourced in such a way that it enables children to take responsibility for 'their' nursery. Everything must have a permanent, clearly marked place. Labelled storage areas ensure that children can quickly see where to return equipment and they take great pride in doing this and great delight in telling when someone gets it wrong. Brooms and mops with short handles enable children to clean up safely (e.g. without poking someone in the eye with long handles), and dustpans and brushes and cloths strategically placed in messier areas encourage them to tidy up for themselves. Of course, children need to be shown how to brush sand into the dustpan, and how to wipe up spilt water with a cloth, but they are remarkably quick learners if shown what to do. In one school, a bucket with a small amount of water and a sponge was placed near the painting easels and children were taught to squeeze out the sponge and wipe down the easel when they had finished painting. This became part of their painting routine and the children generally took great pride in completing this task without getting water on the floor. This pride was encouraged by the staff who praised and encouraged the children's positive achievements and dealt sympathetically with their mistakes.

This approach is based on the belief that children are capable, and that learning to take responsibility does not have to be a battle ground where adults demand and children resist. It also recognizes that some children find taking responsibility harder than others. Many nursery teachers report that girls are keener to be involved in cleaning and tidying than boys. This is perhaps not surprising in view of the adult male and female role models most children see around them. It is therefore important that staff ensure that the willing girls are not always the ones to clean up and that all children see these responsibilities as a part of their life in the class.

Teachers also have to be aware of what can realistically be expected of each child. A new child who has just got out all the bricks would get maximum help from the adult while being expected to be involved in the tidying away process, while an older, experienced child doing the same thing would be expected to clear away with much less support. The important aim is to encourage each child to take at least some responsibility for the consequences of his or her actions and choices.

The main tidying up happens at the end of a session when both staff and children are tired. For this reason plenty of time needs to be given so that the tasks can be undertaken in a relaxed manner, and humour and fun need to be injected into the proceedings. It is amazing how much more willingly all children will get involved in clearing away a huge amount of bricks if an adult approaches the task with enthusiasm and leads them in singing to the tune of 'The farmer's in the den':

> We're clearing up the bricks,
> We're clearing up the bricks,
> Ee ei addy oh,
> We're clearing up the bricks.
>
> Darren's got some square bricks,
> Darren's got some square bricks,
> Ee ei addy oh,
> Darren's got some square bricks.
> (etc. etc.)

Obviously tidying up like this takes longer than if the adult were to do it unaided, but it is time well spent, and by the time children transfer to infant education they are generally very competent and responsible.

Taking responsibility for the environment

The creation of a well organized learning environment is obviously very important if children are to be able to operate independently within it. Children learn to take pride in their environment through the discussions they have with the team while tidying up and cleaning. For example, children who attend for the morning session are encouraged to 'make the nursery look nice for the afternoon children'. As they play they are encouraged to think about actions which may damage or have already damaged equipment: 'Is it a good idea to bury the magnifying glass in the sand? Look what has happened to it.' Nursery teachers realize that young children cannot be expected to know that some equipment is fragile and that they need to explain and discuss the reasons why this is so.

Involving children in ordering equipment, talking about it when it arrives, and explaining that some pieces of equipment cost a lot of money and/or need very careful handling, all help the children to understand something of the cost involved in their education, and of their responsibility in relation to the care of resources. Often though they have to learn the hard way. Being deprived of the cassette recorder for several weeks while it was repaired, because someone had forced all the buttons down at once and jammed the controls, was a powerful learning experience for one class. On its return they were reminded of what had happened and why, and shown again how to use the machine properly. The thought of not being able to listen to story tapes for another long spell was an effective incentive not to mistreat the tape recorder, and older children were observed to be carefully monitoring the behaviour of younger ones.

Obviously this kind of caring attitude towards equipment will only develop if adults in the nursery class act as role models. If no one seems to care whether a puzzle is put away with pieces missing, or that a book is torn or that all the pencils are blunt, then neither will the children. Adults who talk to children about maintenance tasks will encourage them to be vigilant too. They will quickly learn to bring broken equipment to the adults' attention and will enjoy being involved in its repair. If puzzles with missing pieces are left out where everyone is reminded of them, the pieces are much more likely to materialize than if the puzzles are put back on the shelf incomplete.

Through this involvement young children learn a caring, responsible attitude. They learn that equipment has its cost, that there is not an unlimited supply, and that it must be respected and looked after. Nursery teachers are nearly always extremely resourceful. They are often to be found looking in skips and outside shops to see if they can find any safe, useful waste materials for the children to use. This resourcefulness is transferred to the children in the classroom.

A modelling session had come to an end and the teacher was encouraging the children to tidy away a wide range of materials. On the table where the children had been working were several boxes, pieces of cardboard tubing and scraps of paper and fabric. The teacher asked the children to 'think whether any of these pieces are big enough for us to use another day'. She encouraged the children to keep useful junk and throw away any pieces which were too small or too messy with paint and glue. In this way she turned a routine chore into an interesting sorting activity, and encouraged the children's mathematical awareness as well as sharing with them her concern about not being wasteful.

Many teachers are now extending this to involve children in thinking about and improving the environment they live in. For example, involving children in the development of an attractive outside play area helps them to understand that we have the power to improve our environment. Planting flowers, growing vegetables, and picking up litter all help children to take a pride in and take responsibility for their living environment.

Care and respect for living creatures

While investigating and improving their outdoor play space children inevitably come across a variety of small creatures. Some children are afraid of spiders, flies, beetles and so on, and others are fascinated, and want to hold them. Teachers have the opportunity to create a culture where all living creatures are valued by sharing in children's interests and helping them to gain an understanding of the needs of particular insects. For example, an important early lesson is that insects are tiny and our hands are big! Children need to understand that insects can be harmed during handling and that it is best to look at them through a magnifying glass.

If children decide that stamping on insects is fun, then teachers can talk to them about the need to respect life. This can be difficult when many adults see nothing wrong with killing insects – a teacher once had to deal with the father of a new child, who, while settling his son into nursery, led the other children in stamping on the ants in the playground.

The most effective way of fostering respect for living things is to create a natural habitat for insects. Many nursery schools and classes have established 'wild areas' in the grounds where wild flowers and plants are grown to attract butterflies, and where logs and large stones are provided as homes for other insects. Carefully lifting logs and stones provides a structured opportunity for learning about minibeasts, and for talking about the need to respect their home environment.

Some teachers offer children the opportunity to care for pets such as rabbits, guinea-pigs, gerbils or hamsters in the class. This can only be done if staff and parents all understand the need to commit themselves to caring for these animals at school and during the holidays. Children benefit greatly from having the opportunity to take responsibility for the care of a creature much smaller than themselves.

Learning to care for and respect the rights of small creatures is directly relevant to care and respect for other humans. Children are less likely to bully within a caring environment of this kind and more likely to want to care for and help younger, smaller members of their social group. The teacher aims to help children to express their own feelings and empathize with the feelings of others. This is where emotional and social development interlink. Through helping children tune into their own feelings as described in chapter 2, nursery teachers help them to understand the feelings of others. The child who puts an arm around another child, who has fallen and scraped her knee and is crying, and says 'That really hurts doesn't it' is remembering what falling felt like. Similarly, the older child who tells a new child, who has just started to miss her parents and has started to cry, 'You want your mummy don't you? She'll be here in a minute', is probably remembering her own separation experience and realizing how unhappy missing your mum can make you.

This kind of responsibility is both reassuring and empowering. Children are reassured that other children feel as they do, and delight in having the power to offer comfort and support. They are even more delighted when they can offer comfort and support to adults. Often adults try to hide their feelings for fear that small children will be unduly worried. The fact that adults are often not successful is a tribute to the observation skills of young children. They are very quick to notice when adults are behaving differently or when something is wrong. Obviously, there are some worries which it is unwise to share with children, but saying something like 'I didn't sleep very well last night and I feel grumpy this morning' or 'I've got a headache today and the noise you are making is making it worse', reassures children that any change in your behaviour does not mean you do not like them any more, and offers them an opportunity to help by, for example, being quieter.

Learning to play co-operatively

By looking at the ways in which the teacher supports children as they develop the strategies they need to operate in a large social group, we have seen that nursery education is a co-operative venture founded on mutual respect and collective responsibility. Nursery teachers hope that during their time in the nursery, children will learn to play together co-operatively. This does not happen straight away. As Moyles (1989) points out, children may pass 'through a process of spectating, peripheral play and parallel play before engaging fully in social play'.

It is, however, possible for nursery teachers to create an ethos and environment which positively encourages co-operative rather than solitary ventures. Involving children and adults together in projects encourages the view that doing things together is both fun and productive. Creating a 'hill' in an otherwise flat outdoor area involved children, staff and parents in planning and executing a major operation. No one had done such a thing before, so everyone was involved equally in making suggestions and solving problems, and took equal pleasure in the finished result.

Just as large-scale projects need more than one person, so do some pieces of equipment. Nursery teachers consciously select equipment with the aim of encouraging co-operative play. In fact, many will only buy wheeled toys which offer the chance for more than one child at a time to ride.

The strategies required for negotiation have already been discussed. In addition to these skills, children also need to learn how to work together to complete a task. This requires them to be able to make plans together, offer ideas, listen to the ideas of others, and solve problems. Given that many adults have not mastered these skills – witness any course on team building where adults are required to work together to complete a task and see how one or two do it all – and many school-based activities tend to encourage solitary or parallel play (Moyles, 1989), it becomes clear that the teacher has a complex role to play in supporting this learning. She has to help children to take the time to plan what they intend to do including who will do what, encourage them to listen to each other and help them to deal constructively with frustration when things go wrong.

One of the ways to do this is by initiating projects in response to the needs of a small group. A group of four children wanted a 'fridge' in the home corner. Their teacher asked them to think about what they could use to make one, and helped them to work through the process of deciding what to use, and actually making the fridge. She offered support only when needed, and this mainly involved making sure each child's suggestions were listened to, and encouraging them to think in more detail about the features of the model they were making, e.g. at one point she said 'My fridge at home has a special place for putting the eggs. Has yours?' This comment inspired the children to attach an egg box to the inside of the door with Sellotape, and then, because there were no eggs in the home corner, to make some with clay.

This kind of co-operative venture offers a very rich experience and many children demonstrate impressive social ability. Developing social strategies of this kind is a serious business. It involves children in a complex intellectual process, just as coming to terms with feelings does. It is only when the intellectual demands of this kind of learning are understood that the skills involved in nursery teaching are fully appreciated. Teachers know that teaching young children is not just about imparting knowledge or about providing activities or experiences. Most importantly, nursery education involves helping children to develop positive attitudes to themselves and others within the school situation, and learn how to make the most of the opportunities for social interaction. Without these positive attitudes and social competence, they will be less able to take advantage of the full range of opportunities for academic learning on offer to them.

The Need for an Appropriate Curriculum

Some of the components of an appropriate curriculum for young children have already been explored in this and the previous chapter. We have seen how nursery teachers encourage security, self-esteem, self-discipline and positive social interactions. They recognize that the personal and social development of each child is vital to his or her attainment at school, and that they are responsible for creating a positive environment, and for interacting with their pupils in such a way that all children feel valued and encouraged to make progress at their own rate. This does not mean that teachers are not interested in academic curriculum content. As the Early Years Curriculum Group (EYCG, 1989, p. 3) points out 'The early years curriculum is concerned with the child, and the context or setting in which the learning takes place, as well as the content of the learning.'

In recent years, nursery teachers have been forced by a growing body of research (reviewed by Clark, 1988) to reassess their practice in the light of new evidence. For example, Tizard *et al.* (1988) urge nursery teachers to ensure that all children are offered the early literacy experiences they need, and the introduction of the National Curriculum has challenged teachers to demonstrate how the experiences they offer to 3- to 5-year-olds provide a foundation for later learning. When dealing with these challenges, teachers have to remind themselves constantly that young children need a curriculum which is appropriate to their current needs, and that early childhood education is not simply a preparation for the next stage. Only if they keep in mind this and the other principles on which early childhood education is based (Bruce, 1987; EYCG, 1989) can nursery teachers resist the pressure to teach to 'specific but limited targets' (Clark, 1988, p. 278).

How do Young Children Learn?

Young children enter nursery school with a wealth of experience to draw on. Since birth, children have learnt from their interactions with people and their environment. They have already learnt a great deal about the world they live in, and have begun to develop many of the skills they need to operate in their world. As we have seen, it is the task of the teacher to build on this past experience, to recognize and value what children already know and can do, and to support and extend their learning. Clark (1988, p. 278) refers to this process as 'continuity with extension'.

Nursery teachers are in a privileged position which they themselves recognize. They work with children whose spontaneity, natural enthusiasm, curiosity and motivation make them a pleasure to teach. Approaches to the nursery curriculum have developed from observations of the young child's responses to the world they live in. If we watch a group of 3- and 4-year-olds we are given many clues about their learning needs. We see that young children need:

- To be actively (both physically and mentally) involved in first-hand experiences, indoors and out.
- To use their senses to explore the environment.
- To experiment with ways of using equipment, space and time.
- To practise and refine their social and physical skills.
- To talk about their experiences with others.
- To set and solve their own problems (with and without support).
- To observe, question and imitate others.
- To be offered a wide range of materials and experiences and the time to explore them in depth.
- To have access to adults who are interested in their experiences and achievements.

Skilled nursery teachers have used their own observations, and the observations of researchers, to develop a curriculum from these natural qualities and needs. The success with which they have done this has been highlighted by Her Majesty's Inspectorate (DES, 1989a), who have been impressed by the emphasis within nursery education on well-planned, purposeful play which motivates and involves both children and adults. Above all, HMI have confirmed the potential of high-quality play provision to involve children in a broad, balanced curriculum. There is now widespread agreement that young children learn through play and talk (Clark, 1988) and that the early years curriculum must be planned and resourced to provide these experiences.

The Need to Play and Talk

As adults we often forget how important hands-on experience (or play) is for human learning. Yet, if we think about ourselves facing a new piece of equipment for the first time, most of us will admit to pressing a few knobs before consulting the manual or asking someone else. We will also admit that we are most likely to be receptive to learning how to use a new machine when we are motivated to do so (i.e. when we need to use it), and if a more experienced person supports us through the process. Most of us do not grasp things straight away and need time alone to practise and consolidate learning – often through a process of trial and error. We will often want to go back to the experienced person for advice.

For young children, who have considerably less knowledge and understanding of the world than adults, and for whom so much knowledge is new
and exciting and so many physical skills still have to be acquired, the need
for exploration and experimentation is even more important. Play with a
variety of materials provides the perfect vehicle for this learning because it
naturally motivates young children. However, the word play is open to
many interpretations, and nursery and infant teachers regularly complain
that parents and their colleagues teaching older children think it is a soft
option. Nursery teachers have to put up with sarcastic comments like 'have
you had a good morning playing' from colleagues, or 'when is my child
going to do some real work' from parents and, not surprisingly, feel dispirited sometimes.

A simple definition of play has been difficult to come by (Moyles, 1989),
and may not even be a realistic aim (Smith, 1984), but nursery teachers
themselves have demonstrated through their practice, and their increasing
ability to explain their commitment to play, that they recognize its role in
young children's learning. Nursery teachers do not on the whole say things
like 'you can play when you have done your work' (as many infant teachers
have been quoted as saying) – they recognize that play *is* a child's work.

So what is the nursery teacher's perception of the role of play in children's learning? Once again she is influenced as much (if not more) by her
own observations of children responding to the environment she and her
team have created, as she is by research evidence. She has seen for herself
that play is important because it offers children the chance to:

1. *Explore and discover.* During their play, children explore the properties
   of materials, find out how they behave and discover what effect they can
   have on them. This exploration involves all their senses as they handle,
   taste, smell, look at and listen to everything in their environment, and
   encourages the development of a range of physical skills. Young children also explore feelings during play (Hurst, 1991): they discover what
   it feels like to be the baby, mummy, dog, etc., and also get the chance to
   explore their own concerns, such as a hospital visit or the arrival of a
   new baby.
2. *Construct.* Before children can use materials creatively they have to
   learn how to put them together. Children enjoy joining Lego pieces
   together, or sticking paper and boxes together without any particular
   creation in mind. If asked by an adult what they have made they will
   sometimes think for a moment and say what they think the adult wants
   to hear, but it is clear that it is usually the process and not the end
   product which is important to them. Similarly, children construct ideas

about the world they live in based on their own experiences and observations. Listening to these ideas provides nursery teachers with valuable insights into a child's level of understanding.

3. *Repeat and consolidate.* Repetition is an important part of the learning process because it helps us to consolidate our learning. Children will often repeat the same activity over and over again to test out skills – the child who has just completed a jigsaw puzzle for the first time and repeats it over and over again with growing delight, for example.

4. *Represent.* From a very early age children will use one object to represent another in their play, e.g. the rectangular brick used as a telephone. Much of what is required of children during the later stages of education depends on them being able to understand the use of one abstract symbol to represent another – the written word to represent the spoken word, the = sign to represent equals, etc. Young children's early scribbles, which they proudly tell us represent mummy or their name, are important signs of this developing understanding. It is perhaps this aspect of play's potential which is most underestimated with some children (particularly 4-year-olds in reception classes) being expected to cope too early with abstract symbolism (Bennett and Kell, 1989).

5. *Create.* An important development in play occurs when children deliberately use and combine materials to create something they have seen, e.g. a house, car or person. Selecting appropriate materials from the range available and fixing them together involves children in complex physical and intellectual challenges, e.g. how do you stick the tube vertically onto the box so that it does not fall over?

6. *Imagine.* In their play, children take on a whole range of roles and enter a variety of imaginary situations. This kind of play can involve the recreation and exploration of roles and situations within their direct experience, e.g. pretending to be mummy feeding the doll or child baby, and also entry into imaginary situations outside of their first-hand experience, e.g. pretending to cross a crocodile-filled river. Moyles (1989) highlights the value of this kind of play in developing concentration and creative thinking.

7. *Socialize.* Although most children need to explore new materials and experiences alone, and to play in parallel to other children for some time, they find play most challenging when they can talk and interact with others (DES, 1989a) – both with their peers and adults. Earlier in this chapter, we saw how children learn to play co-operatively and the challenges involved in turntaking and sharing. Even greater challenges are involved when children create something together, or make up an elaborate, imaginative game together. It is obvious that children need

language skills in order to be able to socialize in play – perhaps less obvious that they need to play to help them develop the language skills they need. This is because play, especially self-initiated play, inspires talk – witness the frustration on the face of the child who is unable to make herself understood to those she wants to share an exciting experience or discovery with. Play also allows children to take on different social roles – to be in charge, at least for a short time, in an adult dominated world, or to be the baby and to have a safe forum for regression.

In summary, play as a learning process has the potential to fulfil all the nursery teacher's aims for children's development, because it offers a way of motivating and interesting children in a broad curriculum. Play only reaches this full potential, however, if it is carefully planned and resourced, and if the adult has a clear role within it.

The Role of the Teacher in Children's Learning

The role of the adult in children's play has, perhaps, been most misunderstood but also most developed over the years. Nursery education in the 1970s was often dominated by the adult-directed art activity. This involved children in little better than a production line where they filled in outlines, or stuck together junk materials, in ways pre-determined by an adult. One adult was occupied by the activity for most of the session, making sure it was completed satisfactorily by as many children as possible. Apart from its potential as training for the factory conveyer-belt production line, it is difficult to see any educational value in this activity and, certainly, it has nothing to do with creativity (except, perhaps, the adult's). The concentration of adult time on this kind of activity also meant that many curriculum areas were being neglected. HMI (DES, 1989a, p. 9) stress that young children need the same broad range of learning experiences as older children – these experiences should include 'the aesthetic and creative, the human and social, the linguistic and literary, the mathematical, the moral, the physical, the scientific, the spiritual, and the technological'. The introduction of the National Curriculum has further emphasized the need for the teacher to be aware of curriculum content in terms of subject areas.

The approaches to classroom organization and to the children's development as responsible, autonomous learners previously described in this chapter have required teachers and nursery nurses to reassess their roles. Freed from many of the supervisory tasks they used to undertake, they now have considerably more time to observe and listen to children and to extend and support the learning which is taking place, or could take place with support, in play. They have learnt that children learn as much (if not more) from their own self-imposed challenges as they do from those posed by an adult, and that adults can cut across children's self-motivation with insensitive intervention (Bruce, 1987).

The nursery teacher has four main responsibilities when developing the curriculum for 3- to 5-year-olds:

1. She must organize and resource the environment for learning through play and talk.
2. She must demonstrate through her planning and organization her awareness of the potential for cross-curricular learning within the range of experiences she provides – her organization of and plans for experience within the home corner should demonstrate her awareness of the potential for all the areas of learning outlined above, for example.
3. She must use her observations of children responding to the environment she has created to inform her interactions with them and her future planning.
4. She must organize her own and her team's time, so that all children and all areas of experience have access to adult support.

In this chapter, which is concerned with the creation of an ethos and environment for learning, the focus is on organization, resourcing and planning – other areas of responsibility will be explored in following chapters.

Organizing for learning through play and talk

The nursery teacher and her team are responsible for organizing space, equipment and time. There is no doubt that the way they tackle these responsibilities will reflect their priorities and their attitude to young children's learning. Anyone who has ever worked as an advisory teacher or inspector will know that nursery teams working in identical buildings can, and do, create totally different settings for children's learning. Some teams use difficulties associated with the building as an excuse for limiting the provision they make, while others see the same difficulties as a challenge to be tackled and overcome.

Although there can be no blueprint for organizing the learning environment, it is possible to highlight a number of beliefs which are currently informing practice in nursery education. Blenkin and Whitehead (1987, p. 47) stress the need for the learning environment to encourage children's active involvement in their learning – to 'enable them to develop their capacities to act upon the materials which are provided and the situations which they meet in a purposive way'. They also emphasize the need for children to be encouraged by the learning environment to set up their own inquiries and to make independent choices.

This belief in choice, independence and active involvement has motivated teachers to move away from the kind of closed organization where adults select and limit the experiences, to one which emphasizes the child's intrinsic motivation, choice, and partnership between adults and children.

Organizing space and resources

Active involvement requires space both in and out of doors. Nursery teachers recognize that the way in which they lay out their classroom and outdoor area will either facilitate or hinder learning. Classroom sizes and outdoor areas vary, and one of the major challenges for any teacher is how to make the best use of the space available to her and the children. This is why clear principles or beliefs are important – the teacher who believes that young children need to be active will not fill her classroom with tables and chairs, but will set up a range of clearly defined areas of exploration and investigation both in and out of doors.

Children need to have enough room to play alone or with their friends in a purposeful way, but also need some boundaries to help them to learn to take into account the needs of others. Thoughtful use of cupboards and screens, and careful placing of outdoor equipment, ensure that children have the undisturbed opportunities they need for constructive, challenging play. There need to be quiet, relatively secluded areas for children who want to concentrate, or who need the security of a small, enclosed space from which they can observe the rest of the room. There also needs to be provision for safe, large-scale work, e.g. with large bricks, and for challenging physical play.

Teachers need to decide with their team areas of experience to which they want the children to have access, and then work out how they can best make these opportunities available in their own situation. Teams who approach decision-making in this way – starting from what they believe children need and then seeing how this can be put into practice – are likely to achieve more for the children than those who start from the physical environment and allow that to limit their aspirations.

Most nursery classes offer the following range of experiences:

● Opportunities for role play, such as home corner, dressing up, puppets, story props, miniature world equipment, and a range of materials for children to create their own settings for role play, e.g. boxes, blankets, large blocks, milk crates and old steering wheels.

- Opportunities for exploration of the natural environment in and out of doors including sand, water, wood, clay, and earth.
- Opportunities for expressive and creative experience with pencils, pens, paint, fabric, junk materials, and with books, stories, music and movement, etc.
- Opportunities for the continuing development of physical skills, such as climbing, throwing, using a wide range of tools, etc.
- Opportunities for construction and problem solving with bricks made from different materials and of different sizes, a range of construction kits, and junk materials.
- Opportunities for exploration of a wide range of objects and displays, sometimes involving taking something apart, such as an old telephone or radio, and increasingly involving new technology, such as computers and calculators.
- Opportunities for problem solving using a wide range of materials including puzzles, art and craft and construction materials, turntaking games, etc.
- Opportunities for a variety of social interactions – for being active and noisy and for being quiet; for working alone and with others.

When organizing the classroom and outdoor area a workshop approach is often adopted to provide easy access to a full range of materials at all times. In order to consolidate and extend their learning, children need to know that they can return tomorrow to something they were playing with today (Laishley, 1987), and teachers report a dramatic increase in motivation and concentration when children are able to pursue a project or activity over several days at a time.

Although most nursery classes offer a range of provision, the quality of the provision depends very much on the teacher's awareness of the need to maintain resources (both in quantity and condition), and of the importance of adapting and developing the provision in response to the children's use of it (Bruce, 1987). Storage of resources is clearly a prime concern. If children are to make informed choices related to their own learning and to take responsibility for clearing away after themselves, the materials they need must be clearly visible and easily accessible. Low, open drawer units, and stacking storage containers have therefore replaced closed cupboards in many nursery classes.

Organizing time

Stevenson (1987), in her comparison of the experience of 4-year-olds in nursery and infant classes, highlights the constraints imposed on children's activities and on their learning by timetabled interruptions in infant class settings. Nursery teachers, who are now extending the choices available to children, are also offering them more choice in how they use time. Their aim is to enable children to pursue interests at length and in depth, and to decide for themselves when they want to play outside, have their milk or go to the toilet. This, of course, requires them to trust children.

Nursery teachers understand the role of routine in children's lives – that children need to understand the structure of the day so that they can make informed choices rather than random ones. They need to know, for example, that if they start building here now, they will have to clear everything away in 10 minutes because lunch will be served in that area.

The routine in a nursery class should be more concerned with the establishment of flexible daily patterns rather than with set times for whole group activity. A whole class approach is clearly not consistent with a developmental approach where individual needs are of paramount concern – as any teacher who has tried to get the attention of twenty-five 3- and 4-year-olds at story time will confirm.

Because of their varying needs, young children should not be expected to conform within a large group, but should be able to operate at their own pace. A set drink or snack time has been replaced in many classes by a self-service system where children can help themselves when they are thirsty or hungry and when they have reached a convenient time to break away from their activities. Similarly, story times are now less likely to involve the whole class, and more likely to involve members of the team offering stories to smaller groups and to individuals at different points in the day. Nursery teachers who understand children's needs are well able to resist requests from primary colleagues to take the whole class into assembly or PE. They resist because they know that, while it may be appropriate for some of the oldest children who will soon be transferring to infant school to take part in these experiences, it is less appropriate for the younger children to be having these experiences.

Flexible use of time enables all children to develop their own learning styles and patterns. If they are offered real choice within an environment where staff value the full range of activities, children are encouraged to meet their own needs and invariably choose a broad experience for themselves over a period. Adults need to remember that the learning process often requires us to do things over and over again, and to do one thing before we tackle another. No one learns to order, so why is it that we expect children to learn when we make them come and sit down and do something? If our motivation were taken away, and someone else's learning style imposed, we would be unlikely to learn, so why should children be any different?

Some less experienced nursery teachers worry that some children spend too much time at one activity. The answer to this concern is clear. If all areas of experience are planned and resourced to encourage cross-curricular learning, and staff are observing and extending the child's experience and thinking, there is really no problem. What these teachers are really saying is that they think some kinds of experience are less valuable than others – they are unaware of the many kinds of learning which can come from each experience. This attitude effects their approach to these experiences and to the children. By way of a contrast, skilled teachers encourage (through their resourcing and involvement) children to pursue their interests, and inspire them to extend one interest into another. This is explored more fully in Chapters 4 and 5.

Another aspect of time which some teachers worry about is time spent out of doors. Some nursery teachers are still leaving college with only a hazy view of the importance of outdoor play – in spite of the fact that all nursery classes and schools have an outdoor area. Some put their negative attitude into practice by limiting the amount of time children are able to use in the outdoor area. There are many reasons why this is regrettable and they are worth outlining here:

1. Three and 4-year-olds are, of course, growing and gaining control over their body movements. Fine motor skills involving the use of pencils, hammers and rulers are generally acquired later than gross motor skills such as running, jumping and climbing. If we want children to develop one set of skills, we must give them opportunities to develop the others.
2. Young children growing up today are often denied opportunities for safe, outdoor activity. In cities many children live in flats with no garden, and the parks are full of broken glass and dogs' mess, while those living in rural areas are often driven everywhere (ESAC, 1989). In all areas, worries about children being abducted are very real and most parents will not let their children out of their sight. The challenges involved in vigorous outdoor play in the nursery garden are, therefore, more important than ever.
3. The Coronary Prevention Group have warned that even very young children are at risk of heart disease, and that some are already exhibiting signs of predisposing factors (Fletcher, 1988). This is believed to be due

to a lack of exercise and to the increased consumption of junk foods with high fat content. Attention to diet and increased opportunities for physical exercise are recommended.

4. Some learning can only take place out of doors. Work on a large scale, such as construction, painting and role play involving a large group, requires space. Environmental studies, such as gardening, noting and experiencing weather changes, studying living creatures in their natural habitats, are also only possible outside.

5. All other learning can happen as well outside as inside as long as the provision is made for it. For some children who, because of the cramped accommodation they live in, thrive on playing out of doors and are reluctant to come inside, it is vital that rich, cross-curricular provision is made in the outside area. It is certainly not productive to make them come inside – unless we want to make them resentful.

Perhaps we need to stop regarding a nursery class as inside and outside and see it as one learning environment – this is certainly how children see it. Clearly, all teachers need to examine their attitudes and the issues raised here to see if they can really justify the way they organize space, resources and time. The crucial question is: am I organizing for the convenience of staff or to suit our inflexible attitudes, or because of what I know children need?

The teacher's intentions

It is important to stress that the nursery teacher's responsibility goes beyond merely putting out a range of play materials for the children. Through her planning she makes clear her intentions for the children's learning.

When setting up each area of experience she keeps in mind the range of attitudes, knowledge and skills she intends children to learn, and then makes sure that the provision she has made supports that learning. For example, literacy learning will not take place in the home corner if no books or pencils and paper are provided or allowed in that area. However, if memo pads and pens and pencils, telephone directories, newspapers, magazines and other books, empty food boxes and so on are provided, reading and writing experience will be an integral part of the provision. If the teacher also ensures that adults take an interest in the children's developing interest in the written word through their involvement in home corner play, then she gains access to children's levels of understanding and is able to plan for progress. This interaction between planning and assessment is explored in the next chapter.

The Early Years Curriculum Group (EYCG, 1989) have demonstrated through a series of 'webs' how a range of well-resourced play provision can offer the potential for experience within the National Curriculum framework. Many teachers are constructing similar webs, often illustrated with photographs showing children engaged in the full range of activities, demonstrating how the play provision they make offers experience in all subject areas. These webs are being shared with parents and have helped everyone concerned with early learning to understand the importance of children's spontaneous play experiences within a well-planned nursery class.

Only if teachers and their teams have clear intentions for the children's learning will they make rich provision and see the potential for development in children's play. This clarity of intention takes the teacher beyond the role of provider of activities, into the role of learning facilitator. Having clear intentions for learning does not necessarily mean that all children will learn what was intended, but it will offer the best chance of that learning happening.

Many teachers, having observed children beginning to operate autonomously, and use the learning environment in creative ways, have recognized the importance of being flexible and allowing children to move equipment between areas where practical, since in the words of one teacher 'this allows children to create their own broad curriculum'. In this way, children would not be discouraged from filling shopping bags (from the home corner) with junk boxes (from the art and craft workshop area), and taking them outside for a picnic, as long as they put them away again at the end of the session. They would, however, be discouraged from filling the bags with all the lotto game pieces or pieces of a construction set, with the intention of helping children to learn to respect some equipment.

Of course, this kind of flexibility also gives nursery staff clues about their provision – the class where children regularly took dough from the dough table to the home corner was giving their teacher a message about how they wanted to extend home corner play, and the teacher responded by making dough available in the home corner and organizing cooking activities there from time to time.

Balancing group intentions with individual needs

These last examples demonstrate how the teacher, in spite of her intentions, keeps an open mind. It is certainly not her intention to stifle creative thinking or imagination. As we will see in later chapters, one of the pleasures of very young children is their ability to surprise us.

We have seen in this chapter how nursery teachers apply their knowledge and understanding of the needs of young children when they create a learning environment for them. We have seen also the importance of attitudes – both for adults and children. Three-year-olds have not been to school before and teachers are aware that they have the power to enable or deskill their pupils. Curriculum development in recent years has focused on enabling children, and on the creation of the kind of ethos and learning environment which offer all children the chance to reach their full potential. Only if the needs addressed above are taken into account will this happen. These needs must be catered for on both a collective and an individual basis. In this and the previous chapter, the teacher's role in relation to the group has been explored, but it has been made clear that she also has a responsibility to the individuals within that group, and that this requires her to observe and evaluate the provision she makes in the light of what actually happens when children, parents and staff come into contact with it and each other. This will be the subject of the next three chapters.

Some Points for Discussion

Monitoring Adult Behaviour

To what extent are you encouraging children to operate autonomously?

- What is your attitude to the children? Do you really believe they can do things for themselves and take responsibility or, if you are honest, do you do things for them because it is quicker and requires less patience?
- Does your classroom organization encourage autonomy and independence, or does it make children dependent on adults?
- How much of your time is spent doing or getting things for children and/ or telling them what to do? How much of your time is spent observing and listening to them? How much time do you spend explaining/ reasoning/conversing with them? (The best way of discovering the answers to these questions is to ask someone else to observe you.)
- When children are first admitted to your class how do you help them to become aware of:
  - The choices available to them?
  - Their responsibilities such as tidying up, respecting other children, and caring for equipment? The daily routine? The rules for behaviour?
- How do you reinforce this awareness throughout the children's time in your class (particularly after holidays)?
- Are you clear about the kinds of behaviour you wish to encourage? How do you make sure that children are encouraged to behave in these ways,

and guard against unintentionally reinforcing the kinds of behaviour you wish to discourage? (For example, if the aggressive children gain a disproportionate amount of adult attention, it may seem to the other children that this behaviour is worth imitating.)

- Do all adults working in your class work consistently towards the same aims? How do you involve parents in your approach?

Monitoring Children's Behaviour

How autonomous are the children?

- To what extent do children find constructive activities for themselves? Do they use their own initiative or wait to be told/supported?
- Can all children find the equipment they need for themselves or do they have to ask adults? Can they clear away after themselves with/without support?
- Are the children able to use adults as a resource – do they come and ask for help or advice?
- Do all children express their opinions with confidence to adults and to other children?
- Do the children initiate conversations with adults? Do they ask the adults questions? Do they reason things through with an adult?
- Do children negotiate with each other and with adults – or do they dominate or allow themselves to be dominated?
- Do the children play co-operatively and show concern for other children's points of view? Which children can/cannot share and take turns?
- Are certain areas of provision dominated by some children, or are all children confident about using all areas?
- What would happen if you stood back at the beginning of the session and did nothing? Would all children cope? Which children would you need to support and how would you need to support them?

The Provision of Learning Experiences

To what extent does the learning environment you are offering indoors and out encourage children to:

- become actively involved in first-hand experiences?
- engage in sensory exploration?
- set up their own experiments with a wide range of materials and equipment?
- practise and repeat their developing skills?

- work in depth over extended periods of time (including the chance to continue tomorrow something started today)?
- converse and share ideas with other children and adults?
- set and work through their own challenges and problems, observe, ask questions, and learn through imitation of others who have more experience?

What kinds of experiences do you think children should have access to daily, weekly, occasionally? Why? Take a critical look at the provision you are making from the child's point of view - why are things organized in this way? Are you making best use of space, resources and time, i.e. best for children? Can you think of other ways of organizing? To what extent does the learning environment you have created reflect the personal interests and previous experience of the children in your class? How do you ensure that high standards of provision are maintained?

How do you regard the outdoor provision? Do you see it as an extension of the classroom or as a less important area where children 'let off steam'? Ask yourself honestly: what messages are you giving children about the activities you value and those you regard as less important by the provision you make and by your own involvement in activities? How do you encourage all children to take advantage of the broad range of opportunities on offer indoors and out? (Without coercion!) How could you offer a broad, balanced curriculum to those children who choose to spend most of their time out of doors?

How could you use your observations of children more effectively to inform organization?

4
KEEPING RECORDS: – PLANNING AND ASSESSMENT

As teachers have become more aware of the needs of young children, they have been motivated to question and review their approach. Three and 4-year-old children regularly give us strong messages which we can either learn from or ignore.

Thomas, who was nearly 4, was drawing a picture – a rare occurrence – and called me over to see what he was doing. I joined him at the table aiming to involve him in a discussion about his work. I started to talk to him and was delighted to see him apparently listening intently. How quickly my illusion was shattered when he suddenly commented excitedly 'D'you know what? Your nose looks just like a witch's nose!' Our conversation quickly turned to witches and their noses and the aspects of my nose which had made him think of the comparison. There is little hope of retaining vanity in a nursery class! The conversation was more productive than the one I had originally intended, because it captured the child's interest and inspired him to clarify his original idea in more depth.

Anyone who has ever listened to young children could supply similar anecdotes. Our responses to these incidents should give us important messages about our own attitudes to children's learning. The teacher who either ignores the remark or reprimands the child for rudeness, and returns briskly to her original theme, is clearly more concerned with her own intentions than with the child's interests or needs. She subscribes to a transmission model of education where teachers always take the lead and pre-determine the content of the curriculum. Her planning of the curriculum is more concerned with the activities she provides than with the children's possible and actual responses to it. She will assess children in terms of their success or failure at tasks she sets them – often using skills-based checklists.

This approach to education where teachers teach, pupils learn or do not, and teachers tick off attainment may seem attractively simple and clear but, as many nursery and primary teachers are discovering, does not take into account the wonderful spontaneity of young children, i.e. their ability to divert the adult's attention from an activity or conversation they find boring or incomprehensible. Nor does it allow for the child who, in using materials or expressing ideas in unexpected ways, demonstrates levels of thinking way beyond our expectations.

Perhaps most importantly it does not take into account the questions raised by research (Tizard and Hughes, 1984; Wells, 1986; Bennett and Kell, 1989) concerning teachers' ability to provide meaningful learning experiences which will inspire and bring out the full potential in each child. The message from research has been clear – just because teachers offer learning experiences does not necessarily mean that children will learn, and just because children do not seem to learn in one context does not mean they are incapable of learning. Research has confirmed that teachers must observe and listen to children to challenge their own assumptions, and to enable them to make a better match between the curriculum they offer and the developmental needs and current interests of individual children. If they do not do this they run the risk of switching children off from learning (NFER/SCDC, 1987).

A Developmental Approach

Curriculum development for teachers has been concerned with an exploration of the implications of research for practice. In accepting a developmental approach to the curriculum for young children, the highest priority must be given to the needs and development of the individual child, and the limitations of the teacher must be recognized. This requires the teacher to be humble and to value the contribution each child makes – to recognize that she does not have a monopoly on knowledge about children, or about the kind of approach to learning which will work best for an individual child, and that she can gain clues from other adults who know the child, and from the child.

Teachers also need to remember that their own learning will have been inhibited in important ways, which may limit their view of the possibilities for learning available to children. For example, many teachers say that their own negative feelings about subjects such as science can limit their approach to children's learning in this area. They also say that exploring and discovering alongside young children has been the most effective science teaching they have received.

A developmental approach is, therefore, concerned with opening up our perception of children, of learning, and of teaching, and requires us to accept that our own view is likely to be a narrow one. It demands that we learn from others (both adults and children), and that we regularly test out through observation our assumptions about children and the provision we make. It is not surprising that the role of recordkeeper is such a prominent one in the life of the nursery teacher.

Teachers and nursery nurses are trained to observe and to learn from observation. Their approach to recordkeeping has inspired other teachers in the primary phase and has been incorporated into published records such as *The Primary Language Record Handbook* (Barrs *et al.*, 1988). What is so remarkable about the best teachers is that, in spite of their acknowledged skill, they are not satisfied with their achievements and are still intent on improving their practice. Many feel that although they have developed ways of keeping a variety of records, they need to review their purposes in the light of new evidence, and to make sure that their methods actually serve these purposes.

Why Keep Records?

This is a question which many groups of nursery teachers have been addressing. Their answers, collected on in-service courses, demonstrate their awareness of the complex nature of their job, and of the need to broaden the scope of their recordkeeping. Their answers can be grouped into six main areas:

1. *To find out about children as individuals.* This will lead to a deeper understanding of each child's learning style, interests, developmental characteristics and to the identification of any special educational needs. Teachers aim to gain a more objective view of each child and recognize that they benefit from having other adults in the team who relate to the children differently and can challenge their thinking.
2. *To monitor the progress (or lack of it) of individual children.* A major concern for all teachers is that the children they teach should make progress whatever their starting point. It is therefore necessary to review regularly children's achievements in order that plans can be made to support progress.

3. *To inform curriculum planning.* Planning and assessment are interrelated and teachers are trying to ensure that one influences the other. In order to develop an appropriate curriculum which meets the needs of the group as well as individual needs, teachers need to discover how the curriculum they have offered has been received and to use this information to help them plan future approaches. In this way, recordkeeping highlights the difference between the intended and the received curriculum – the difference between what teachers plan for children to learn, and what children actually learn. Teachers must make themselves aware of this inevitable difference if they are seriously interested in children as individuals who learn at different rates and in different ways and, therefore, require a variety of approaches.

4. *To enable staff to evaluate the provision they make.* If curriculum planning is to be responsive in the ways suggested above, the teacher needs to know how effectively she and her team are working with the children. Concern about equality of opportunity has increased awareness, and many teachers are now monitoring their policies and practice in order to identify inequalities.

5. *To provide a focus for communication with others.* Because they work in a team, teachers have always seen the potential of records for opening up communication with other adults such as nursery nurses, parents, speech therapists and infant teachers, and with the children. It is clear that they see recordkeeping as a shared initiative which everyone can contribute to. Increasingly, in common with other teachers, nursery teachers see records in terms of accountability - a way of explaining and justifying their work to others who have the right to ask.

6. *To make the job more enjoyable.* Many teachers feel that their work is enlivened by the need to keep records. They positively enjoy finding out about and talking about children. Children make the job worthwhile and provide, through their unexpected responses to adults and materials, the intellectual challenges which make nursery teaching the exciting, collaborative venture it undoubtedly is.

What Information Should Records Contain?

Many teams have identified the strengths and weaknesses of their current practice, discovering that they need to be clear about the kinds of information the purposes outlined above require them to collect. A major potential weakness of any recordkeeping system is an over-concentration on some children or some aspects of development at the expense of others. The first step towards overcoming this weakness is for all members of the team to be clear about what is to be recorded for each child, since only then can gaps be identified.

Taking the above issues into account, teachers are making their teams aware of the need to keep a record of:

1. Each child's experience prior to school entry.
2. The provision which is made both for groups of children and individuals (including physical provision and materials, and adult involvement).
3. Each child's social, emotional, physical, and intellectual responses to the nursery experience – those aspects of development outlined in Chapters 2 and 3.
4. The use of the available provision by the group as a whole (particularly noting whether children gain equal access to the curriculum on offer).
5. Each child's developing knowledge, skills and understanding – what children know and can do at particular points in time.

This information provides the basis from which nursery teams can plan, implement and evaluate their practice and each child's experience.

Who Should Contribute to the Records?

If she is to gain access to the types of information listed above, the teacher needs to encourage all members of the team to contribute to the children's records. Young children come into contact with a wide range of adults both before and after starting nursery school, all of whom have a perception of the child. Before admission to nursery class, these adults could include parents and other close relatives, childminders or nannies, day nursery, playgroup or toddler club staff, health visitors, social workers, speech therapists and GPs; while after admission adults such as supply staff, students, headteachers, part-time support staff, meals supervisors, educational psychologists, school nurses and doctors could be involved alongside teachers and nursery nurses.

While recognizing that all of these adults may have valuable information to offer, the logistics of involving so many people in recordkeeping leaves the teacher with a difficult, if not impossible, task. How each one makes a contribution will depend on who they are, and on the involvement they have had with the child. All the teacher can realistically do is get to know who is involved with each child, and create the kind of atmosphere and opportunities which would encourage the sharing of information.

Experience demonstrates that the teacher who shares her ideas and shows that she is interested in the ideas of others is likely to gain the broadest view of the children in her class. Above all, she must accept that others have a valid point of view. If a teacher believes that parents cannot be trusted to tell the truth about their child, she closes off the possibility of finding out what the child does at home – and, in any case, there is almost certainly going to be more than one 'truth' for each child. We know from research (Tizard and Hughes, 1984; Wells, 1986) that children often demonstrate skills at home which they never display at school.

Just as parents like to hear about their child's achievements at school, so should teachers be keen to hear about the children's home and community experience. Hurst (1987, p. 101) stresses that 'teachers need to involve parents in their children's education in school because without this connection between home and school schooling can become cut off from the child's deepest and most influential experiences'.

Whomever she involves in recordkeeping, the teacher always has overall responsibility for ensuring that appropriate, meaningful information is collected, and that the contributions of all adults are valued and included, e.g. she is responsible for adding comments given verbally to the child's written records.

Increasingly, teachers are also valuing the children's viewpoints, and are noting comments which they make about their work or about their interactions with adults. It is particularly important that nursery staff listen to children when child abuse is suspected, since a child's comments may confirm that a bruise or burn the staff have noticed was not an accident and requires further investigation. As we saw in the last chapter, teachers need to ensure that the atmosphere they have created encourages this kind of sharing of confidences. Certainly, a collective, partnership approach to recordkeeping is likely to result in a rounder, more flexible view of children than a solo approach.

This is a potential weakness of a system where each member of the basic nursery team takes responsibility for the records for a set number of children. This approach can lead to a possessive view of children and a tendency not to focus on those children 'who are not one of mine', and thereby loses the advantages which are gained when adults challenge each other's perceptions. One of the most valuable experiences available is for several adults to observe the same incident in the nursery class, and then to discuss what they saw and how they interpreted what they saw. Not only will each adult see the incident differently (each one focusing on different parts of it), but they may also interpret the same events differently according to their own values and attitudes. In sharing these differences in perception, adults come to a deeper understanding of children and of themselves – and in the process become less sure that anything involving young children can be certain. Perhaps this experience should be made available to local and national educational policy-makers. It might challenge the oversimplified view of young children they sometimes hold.

How can Information be Recorded?

Most nursery teams have worked hard to develop methods of recordkeeping which suit their purposes and which they can manage. In developing their approach, they have taken note of published material such as the *Keele Preschool Assessment Guide* (Tyler, 1979) and *The Primary Language Record Handbook* (Barrs *et al.*, 1988), local authority guidelines and methods adopted by colleagues in other nurseries; but most feel that the work involved in developing their own methods is vital to the team's commitment to them.

In any case, no one method or combination of methods could necessarily serve the many different types of nursery class. One teacher, who had recently taken a post in a double, open plan nursery unit with two teachers and two nursery nurses, commented that her recordkeeping had 'gone to pot'. She went on to explain that in her previous post she had been responsible for a class of mainly full-time children, and had been able to develop what she felt were comprehensive and useful records. In her new position where the majority of children attended part time (resulting in large numbers passing through the class every day), it was impossible to keep up with her old methods and she was having to think again. She was deeply disappointed to discover that she no longer felt efficient, and yet the problem she was facing was very real.

There are lessons here for those responsible for nursery class admissions. It may seem like a good idea to double the numbers of children able to attend by offering mostly, or exclusively, part-time places, but in terms of quality recordkeeping and curriculum planning based on children's needs, this arrangement presents often insuperable problems to the nursery team. Teachers would be relieved to discover that their difficulties were acknowledged, especially since many of them already use a range of methods of recordkeeping without rival in the education system. They are generally not content with one method of recording, preferring to adopt the widest possible range of strategies. They are also the pioneers as far as involving parents in recordkeeping is concerned.

The methods currently in use are briefly as follows:

1. Profiles of each child completed before admission to nursery class in conjunction with parents and others who have known the child well.
2. Written observations stored in a loose-leaf folder with a section for each child, or on index cards.

3. Dated samples of work, photographs or tape recordings with written comments giving contextual information and providing a record of the children's experience and progress.
4. Checklists to record developmental achievements, children's involvement in activities, e.g. how often a child uses sand, books, etc., or takes part in cooking or other group activities, and adult involvement in activities and with children.
5. Regular summaries of children's achievements providing a profile of the child at a particular point in time, and identifying the support which could be offered to facilitate progress – these profiles are often used as a focus for discussion with parents and others interested in the child's development.

The Importance of Observation

Observation is the key to all these approaches. The effectiveness of any of them relies on the teacher's ability to:

- Observe each child as an individual and as part of the group.
- Analyse and evaluate each observation (Hurst, 1991).
- Identify the significant aspects of each observation.
- Use the information gained to inform her approach to each child.

The teacher acts as a role model for the rest of her team and encourages others, including parents, to observe and learn from the children (Athey, 1990). She is aware of the need to stand back sometimes from what is happening (even if only for a couple of minutes each day), and write down as objectively as possible what takes place and what is said. These focused observations provide a challenge to assumptions because they provide information which might otherwise be missed.

Maria (3½ years) had been considered by the nursery team to be a well-adjusted, independent child who was well able to occupy herself. It was only when the nursery teacher instigated a series of time sampling observations (involving listing which children and adults were involved in each area of learning at 15-minute intervals) to find out how the various areas of learning were being used, that it was noticed that Maria was always on the edges of activity and never seemed to be involved. Focused observation of Maria over the next few days confirmed that she was having difficulty making contact with other children and adults and, therefore, remained alongside them. With this information the team were all made aware of Maria's needs and were able to discuss strategies to help her. All teachers know that quiet children are at risk of being overlooked in the busy class situation. Focused observation is the only way of preventing this from happening. Dowling (1988, p. 121) describes a number of useful methods of focused observation which can be built into the daily routine.

Obviously, it is not always possible to stand back and observe in this focused way. Neither is focused observation the only way of observing. Nursery staff regularly comment that they are 'observing all the time'. There is some truth in this comment, but it also requires qualification. What nursery teachers and nursery nurses do all the time is notice the things which draw themselves to their attention – the cry or laugh, the wonderful construction, the child who speaks to them for the first time, the fight over a toy, the child happily saying goodbye to mum, dad or minder for the first time, and so on. These are important happenings to notice and record, but they are not the complete picture. What about all those things which happen quietly – the wonderful drawing completed without reference to an adult which goes straight into a pocket for mummy, the subtle, verbal bullying by the child who knows better than to let an adult hear, the sexist comment during home corner play, or the incident which led up to the cry?

It is frustrating to acknowledge that we will never see or hear everything that happens. However, we can sharpen our observation skills through the more focused kind of observation described above. Through standing back and seeing more of the total picture, we make ourselves more aware of the possibilities. Teachers who have been asked to make focused written observations as part of a course often report how much more they are now noticing incidentally. The discipline involved in writing down as far as possible what they see and hear happening, opens their eyes and ears, and enables them to see and hear more even when they are not particularly looking or listening.

This is why observation and discussion of observations form a vital part of initial training courses. Sadly, some students on both teacher and nursery nurse training courses start their first post believing they can now forget about observation. They have not been helped to see the purpose of observation and do not realize that everything (particularly their record-keeping) depends on it. Above all, they have not realized that their work will be more enjoyable if they take the time to study the children. In-service training courses should therefore re-emphasize the importance of observation as an essential, integral part of nursery education.

The Recordkeeping Process

Keeping records is a complex activity and involves considerably more than simply ticking off skills and knowledge. The remainder of this chapter is concerned with the process involved and some insight into this process in action.

The recordkeeping process cannot be seen as a simple step-by-step model. It is more appropriate to see it as a meandering activity, integrating curriculum planning and assessment, with stages having to be revisited as necessary. Even though they cannot be placed in a fixed, sequential order, it is possible to identify the component parts of the process, all of which have already been identified in this chapter.

Teachers and their teams are required to:

- Find out about children – both as typical 3- and 4-year-olds and as unique individuals.
- Make plans which reflect their intentions for learning – for the group as a whole and for individuals.
- Implement the plans.
- Monitor and note what actually happens – how children respond to the provision which has been made for them.
- Identify and record children's achievements and regularly review each child's progress.
- Share perceptions with others and, on the basis of all information, evaluate what has taken place or what an individual child needs.
- Plan again to find out more about children and to improve provision.

Recordkeeping in Action

Finding out about Children – A General View

Teachers extend their knowledge of young children during their initial training course through their study of child development, and through their own observations on teaching practice. Whether future students will have the chance to study in the same way is debatable, since the new requirements for teacher training courses, which place more emphasis on the study of academic subjects, may lead to a squeezing out of child development much to the dismay of early years tutors.

In any case, however intensive their study of children during initial training, teachers still have a great deal to learn. Nursery teaching is quite simply about studying children and about continuing to study them throughout your career. There are two related parts to this study. First, teachers need to understand about children in general – ideally from birth until at least 7. They need to know the kinds of things 1- to 7-year-olds typically do, say, and think, and the kinds of behaviour patterns which can be expected, along with some of the possible reasons for this development. They need to understand environmental, sociological and psychological theories, in order that their view of society is broadened, and is taken beyond their own limited life experience. This latter kind of study is currently under threat, again being squeezed out by subjects considered to be more important by those who believe that education is merely about imparting knowledge, and does not include an understanding of human development.

They also need to know that development is an individual process, and that the general picture is only a rough guide. Individual children develop uniquely, and a wide range of behaviour and actions can be considered 'normal'. Throughout their career, teachers must continue to learn about 3- and 4-year-olds by informing their general view of children through the study of individuals.

The most committed teachers are addicted to child study. In addition to studying the children in their class, they read about children (in novels, newspapers and magazines), they find themselves compulsively watching children in the neighbourhood (on buses, in the park, etc.) and on television, and they talk with other nursery teachers about children (even after in-service courses which finish after 6.00 p.m.!). In this way, they build up their knowledge of children in general and are better equipped to understand the individuals in their class.

This general knowledge and understanding is essential for the development of a set of principles and beliefs which underpins effective work with young children. The growing number of inappropriately trained teachers now working in nursery classes is therefore a major cause of concern – if you do not know about children how can you provide appropriately for them? Theoretical study of child development, backed up by experience with, and observation of, young children is the only way to provide a firm foundation for the teacher.

For example, if we turn our attention again to Natalie (introduced briefly in Chapter 2) and think about her excited 'babbling' on the telephone, and her temper tantrums when she could not make herself understood, we see that the two aspects of her behaviour are linked. Her language development was at a level usually associated with a much younger child – a 2-year-old. It is no coincidence that we sometimes refer to the 'terrible 2s' since this is the stage when temper tantrums are common. They are common at this age because the 2-year-old is at a very early stage of language development and wants to express much more than she can say. Natalie's tantrums were consistent with her language development and with her frustration at not being able to communicate effectively with others. She needed, and was given, help in this area, and as her communication skills developed the temper tantrums decreased. Attempting to tackle the tantrums without understanding the cause would have been futile. A knowledge of how 2-year-olds are helped to acquire speech gave the nursery team clues for their involvement – in particular, it helped them to understand the kinds of experiences Natalie might have missed.

Theory without practice is as inadequate as practice without theory. The first may place too much emphasis on norms at the expense of the individual, while the second provides no base from which to assess individual behaviour and development, and may not provide the necessary challenge to our own view of human behaviour.

Finding out about Children – As Unique Individuals

As we saw in Chapter 2, teachers begin to find out about individual children before they are admitted to nursery class, by way of parents and others who have been involved with the child in the process. They regard the information which they collect at this early stage as the beginning of the child's school record, and use the information to help them adapt the curriculum they offer to the needs of each child. They do this because they recognize that children starting nursery class do not have a shared, common, previous experience in the way that a class of 7-year-olds have had when they move to the next class, and because they recognize their responsibility to consider each child as a whole person in the way described in the previous two chapters.

Each team, in consultation with parents, who often have very strong views about what they wish to tell the nursery staff, will decide what information would be useful to them and how they will record it. This information usually includes basic details such as date of birth, names of carers, number of siblings, language(s) spoken at home, religion, playgroup or toddler group experience, and health details such as allergies, chronic illnesses (e.g. asthma) and contact with specialists and their names. This information may be recorded on the form completed by the parent when they apply for a nursery place.

More detailed information is also considered useful and is often collected during a home visit or when the child and parent make an initial visit to the nursery class or toddler group (if there is one). This may include the following details about the child:

1. Life history:
   (a) what the child was like as a baby/toddler,

(b) her relationships with other children and other adults,

(c) any stressful experiences such as hospitalization, new baby, death in the family, house move etc.,

(d) details of previous pre-school group experience or child care – how the child settled, how often she attended, what she likes/dislikes about the group, and so on,

(e) the child's eating habits including what she likes and dislikes, foods which disagree with her, what cutlery she uses, etc.,

(f) the child's involvement in religious and cultural activities.

2. Development:

(a) physical skills, and physical activities, e.g. can she ride a bike, does she use the toilet unaided, can she dress herself, what opportunities has she had to play in a large space, to go to the park or swimming pool, etc.,

(b) language competence both in English and the language(s) spoken at home, any family words used, e.g. for going to the toilet,

(c) what the child likes to play with and how she spends her time, and any special interests or skills,

(d) social skills including how the parents think she will relate to children and adults at the nursery, and any children she already knows,

(e) the child's emotional development including any fears and anxieties, what frustrates or angers the child and how the parent deals with the child when she is angry; any special toys or comfort objects.

Teachers negotiate with the parent which information is written down and the parent is often asked to sign it to ensure accuracy. In the case of bilingual parents and children, teachers try to ensure that an interpreter is available to give these families an equal opportunity to share information.

A consistent approach to the collection of information is vital, particularly if both teachers and nursery nurses are involved in the process. Parents need to feel confident that their views are positively respected, and that value judgements about them as parents, about their home (in the case of home visits), or about their child will be avoided. A structured approach where all members of staff work from the same set of questions or headings, which parents are shown in advance, helps to allay any fears a parent may have. Some teachers are offering parents the opportunity to complete the *All About Me* profile developed by Wolfendale (1987), and encouraging them to share this with school staff.

Teachers will also want to make contact with any playgroup or day nursery the child has attended to gain the staff's perceptions of the child's experience in these settings, to see for themselves how the child operates there, and to identify any areas of discontinuity which may make transfer confusing or stressful for the child.

Many teachers establish, through visits and the local discussion group, close contact with staff working in other forms of statutory and voluntary provision for the under-5s. Where these kinds of contacts have been set up, visits between the various establishments and discussions about children, who are transferring from one group to another, are a natural extension. Some workers, particularly day nursery officers, pass on a written summary of the child's experience, and this would be added to the child's school record. Where views are communicated verbally, the teacher is responsible for adding the main points to the child's record.

In this way, teachers and their teams begin to find out about children as unique individuals who have a wealth of experience. Without this information the team would be unable to claim to be aiming for a match between each child's needs and the curriculum offered (Lally, 1989b).

Making Curriculum Plans

Curriculum planning has been evolving to take into account the developments outlined above – in particular the need to plan responsively for the group as a whole and also for the learning of individuals within the group. It is no longer considered appropriate merely to produce a timetable of activities for the day or week, since this type of planning implies (through its exclusive focus on what is to be provided rather than what might be learnt) a delivery approach to teaching, and does not make clear the teacher's intentions for learning. Neither does it take into account the children's individual stages of development, and the need to differentiate the curriculum according to each child's needs and interests.

Some teachers actually used to claim not to plan because they 'follow the children's interests'. With the need for greater accountability, these teachers have had to think again, and it is not surprising that they have found the process difficult.

In reviewing their approach to planning the curriculum, it has been necessary for all teachers to develop methods to meet their new purposes. Clearly, careful planning is required if all children are to:

- operate as self-motivated, independent learners,
- gain relevant, meaningful experiences,
- be offered equal opportunities,

- gain access to a broad, balanced, differentiated curriculum,
- have access to adult time.

Planning is also necessary to ensure that adult time is used productively, and to enable all members of the team to work effectively with the children. Clift, Cleave and Griffin (1980) discovered that interactions between nursery staff and children were often fleeting and lacked the kind of depth which would lead to the children's learning being extended. Teachers have realized that only with careful planning will they be able to avoid this problem.

These complex reasons for planning necessitate a varied approach, and teachers are currently struggling to develop planning methods which are meaningful, manageable, and useful and which are true to their principles. Many (particularly those working in nursery classes attached to primary schools) believe that the focus on whole school planning, and the emphasis on planning to account for National Curriculum coverage have added further complications. Teachers have reported that they feel unhappy about being required to follow a whole school theme which is closely linked to attainment targets, because they believe it takes them back to the unrealistic, meaningless methods of the past. They believe that an over-emphasis on subject content will make it more difficult to plan a responsive approach to individual needs (Lally, 1989a).

The crucial questions for all teachers to address honestly are: Are we planning for delivery or for learning? Are we more concerned with our intentions or about children's responses? There is, of course, no clear cut answer to these questions, since teachers need to plan and be concerned about both sides of the teaching and learning equation – but one side should not dominate at the expense of the other.

One way of simplifying the problem has been to think in terms of long-term and short-term planning, and in terms of learning possibilities and learning outcomes. This approach seems to address the anxiety expressed by many nursery teachers that planning could lead to a loss of spontaneity in their work. They believe that they need to be free to grasp the moment at the point when a discovery has been made or an interest shown, because they believe that it is then that learning is most likely to happen. They also argue (and quote evidence from amongst others Holt (1970); Tizard and Hughes (1984); Wells (1986); and Hughes (1986) to support their argument) that, if meaningful contexts (ones which are interesting to the child) are essential to motivate children, they must adopt a flexible approach to curriculum planning and cannot be expected to predict up to a year in advance what will be meaningful. This argument is valid but, nevertheless, there are flaws in it as we shall see when we explore the planning options available to the nursery teacher.

Long-term planning – curriculum policy development

The importance of the teacher's intentions for children's learning, and the relationship between the clarity of these intentions and the quality of the learning environment, were stressed in the previous chapter. Blenkin and Whitehead (1987, p. 35) point out that 'the most neglected and misunderstood dimension of the planned curriculum is the creation of an environment or setting in which education is to take place'. In recent years, as schools have developed curriculum policy statements, the relationship between the quality of learning and the environment in which that learning takes place has been realized.

Teachers are seeing the value of working with their team to put their intentions down on paper. Very often an early part of this process is an analysis of the learning which they hope will take place as children work in particular areas, and an identification of the resources which would be needed to support that development.

Two main approaches to this task have emerged. Teams either start from an area of provision, such as the home corner or the block area, listing the kinds of resources available, and working out what cross-curricular learning may result from experience within this area; or they start from an area of learning, such as mathematics or personal and social development, and examine all areas of provision in order to identify the possibilities for this kind of learning. The Early Years Curriculum Group (EYCG, 1989) illustrate these two approaches through web diagrams, although the focus on the National Curriculum limited the scope of these diagrams to some extent. For example, the web related to the home corner illustrates only how the core curriculum and technology are covered and does not (except incidentally) include areas of learning such as art, music, history, personal and social development.

Teams are also seeking to ensure that opportunities for progression in learning are made available through careful resourcing of areas, e.g. is the collection of jigsaw puzzles organized in such a way that all children can select some which they can complete easily, some which they can complete with support from an adult or a more experienced child, and some which they can aspire to? It is clear here that staff need to plan how they will help children to make these informed choices and to use the learning environment productively.

Teams which have written up the results of their discussions in detail have set themselves a standard, and are usually well equipped to monitor their provision. If they have clearly defined their expectations for each area of provision and each area of learning, and for the children's ability to make use of this provision, they will be able to check that high standards are maintained and to evaluate the extent to which their intentions are being achieved in practice. These teams report that their perception of learning possibilities has been broadened and they feel more confident about supporting children's learning across the curriculum and in all subject areas.

This is probably because the broader our view of learning possibilities, the more likely we are to see opportunities for stimulating children's interest, and the more likely we are to accept individual responses to provision rather than impose our own narrow ideas. We are much more likely to be able to accept a child who uses the provision we make in an unexpected way, or who diverts us from our cause with a well-timed intervention, if we are aware that there is potential for learning in virtually all experiences. Whether any learning at all takes place often depends on adults having a flexible approach, and being able to see when children need something other than that which has been provided.

A further spin-off from these written statements is that parents can be given access to them, and to discussions/workshop sessions based on them, and are increasingly understanding the role of the activities on offer to their children.

In the absence of clear intentions and expectations, provision can become static, and standards may slip without anyone realizing the significance for children's learning. For example, if staff do not clarify that children need a full set of plates, mugs and cutlery to enable them to set the table and develop mathematical concepts, such as one-to-one correspondence (one plate, mug, cutlery set for each child), and addition and subtraction ('I've got two plates. How many more do I need for the four dolls?'), they may not see the importance of replacing broken or missing items. Very quickly the home corner degenerates and the quality of play and learning is adversely affected.

Long-term planning - planning for spontaneous happenings

This heading sounds like a contradiction in terms and in some ways it is. It is the intention in this section to challenge those teachers who feel planning gets in the way of a responsive approach to spontaneous happenings.

Many of the things which nursery staff see as spontaneous happenings or interests are, in fact, absolutely predictable. Using their knowledge of children in general, they know that during a typical year children's interest will at some point be captured by events, such as a windy or even a snowy day, someone's new baby, a weekend visit to the park or zoo, a long journey or holiday to visit a relative, an interesting object someone has brought to school, a 'plague' of creatures (ants, or worms after rain), a bird building a nest in the school guttering, the building site or hole in the road visible from the school playground – the list is endless.

If teachers are to be able to respond in depth to these interests when they happen, they need to have organized their thoughts and resources in advance. There is absolutely no point in trying to teach young children about the properties of snow when there is no snow in sight, and yet how often are children asked to represent snow with cotton wool just because it is December or January? This is the classic example of activity planning taking precedence over learning intentions or even sense! After all, what does the use of cotton wool teach children about snow? And, of course, by the time snow comes in April, the books have been returned to the library!

In the changing British climate it is essential to take advantage of the very occasional day when there is a flurry of snow. Unless this eventuality has been considered and prepared for, the snow will have melted by the time teachers have gone to the library for books, or sorted out the outdoor spades, or decided what possibilities there are for exploring snow. Young children's interests will not always wait for us to catch up with them. Through their response, teachers have the power to capture and develop interest, or to turn children's attention to something else. As role models they encourage (or discourage) nursery nurses and the children's parents to be more aware of the value of following up events in this way.

Although it is not possible to say in advance if or when it will snow, or when exactly a new baby will be born, it is possible to say what could be done about these happenings if they occur. Teachers, rather than feeling they have to come up with plans for a topic or theme for a whole year or even a term (which is often peripheral to the children's real interests), could instead think about the kinds of things they know are likely to generate interest, and plan for extending these interests. These plans could, again, take the form of web diagrams (stored in a loose-leaf folder for easy reference), which demonstrate how the starting point or interest could be developed across the curriculum and what resources would be needed to support each learning possibility. Links with the National Curriculum programmes of study could be added in order to make staff and parents aware of the potential for learning from everyday interests. Written plans of this kind would be meaningful, and could be drawn on and implemented when an interest is shown.

Written long-term plans of this kind would also enable staff to check that resources are available and stored in such a way that they are easily accessible when the need arises. For example, books about different kinds of weather could be bought and stored together to be introduced when appropriate, and boxes or drawers containing resources relevant to particular interests, e.g. a box relevant to babies could contain feeding equipment, a selection of baby clothes, pictures or photographs (perhaps of the staff as babies) and so on, could be collected and labelled. This is not to say that resources of this kind should not always be available to the children – obviously, young children have a general (as well as a specific) interest in babies, and will want to pursue this during their home corner play, where baby dolls, clothes and feeding equipment should be available. However, it is also important to have some special resources available to stimulate and extend specific interests.

Planning from a range of starting points in this way is time consuming but, once accomplished, only needs occasional updating in the light of experience. In fact, teachers and nursery nurses from several classes could be encouraged to work together on in-service courses to develop plans, with lists of supporting resources, and would undoubtedly benefit from the inevitable cross-fertilization of ideas. Above all, it would encourage all adults to access, and work from, their general knowledge of young children, and the potential for learning from each other would be very high.

Long-term planning is concerned primarily with the identification of learning possibilities, and with ensuring that the environment offered is consistent with these possibilities – that it supports our learning intentions and offers children the chance to pursue their interests.

However, when we identify that it is possible for children to learn about writing through use of pens and memo pads in the home corner, or about forces on a windy day, we are not able to say when this learning will take place for an individual child, or what exactly each child will learn. The child in the home corner although using the pencil and memo pad may be using them to make drumming sounds, and the child playing out on a windy day may be most concerned about Adam not being his friend. Just because the provision has been made, does not mean that all or any children will be motivated to use it in the ways we have intended.

This is why long-term planning must be accompanied by short-term plans which take into account the needs, developing interests and achievements of individual children.

Short-term planning

Long-term plans are based on the general needs of young children and act as a guide to remind teachers of the range and depth of curricular experiences they need to offer. Using these plans teachers are able to set up the learning environment and monitor its effectiveness. Short-term plans, made on a weekly basis, and evaluated and amended daily, encourage a more responsive approach to the curriculum for individual children, and provide a more accurate record of teaching and learning.

As teams gain information about individual children, from others who know the child and from their own observations of each child in the school setting, they are able to use it to inform their curriculum planning, and make the provision they offer more relevant to specific needs. This responsive approach to curriculum planning involves teachers in highlighting with their team the need to:

- Help new children settle into the nursery class.
- Enable all children to operate confidently within the nursery environment and to develop attitudes and skills described in Chapters 2 and 3.
- Enable children to extend their personal interests.
- Provide challenges for experienced or particularly able children.
- Support the development of children with special educational needs.
- Support children who are experiencing emotional difficulties.
- Enable children to take part in group activities.

In order to meet, or attempt to meet, the wide range of needs within the class, teams must make full use of their focused and informal observations. Their focused observations ensure that each child is regularly the centre of their attention, while their informal observations enable them to pick up on daily incidents of note which are worthy of extension. Both of these methods of observation provide the team with information about individual children, about small groups, and about the group as a whole.

It would be naïve to suggest that any one method of recording curriculum plans were the most appropriate. This aspect of curriculum development is the subject of much debate. Teachers attending courses always ask for a discussion of planning to be included, emphasizing the difficulties involved. However, it is possible to suggest what could be included in weekly plans, based on current developments in practice.

Having worked out her long-term plans the teacher needs to turn her attention to her specific intentions for a particular week and day. These intentions will include:

1. *Plans for the learning of individual children including the addition of resources to extend learning.* Examples of this kind of planning might include notes such as:

- Spend time at beginning of session with new children (particularly Jodie and Darren) to help them select resources more confidently.
- Suggest to Adam that he finds books on spiders to develop the interest he was showing in webs yesterday.
- Work with Elena and Matthew at tidying up time to encourage them to see this as fun rather than as something to be avoided.
- Introduce bottles with holes pierced at different levels to extend bottle filling activity which Sam and Claudette have been interested in for the past few days. Encourage talk about the rate at which different bottles empty and why.
- Add first-aid kit to home corner in response to Gemma's play yesterday (seen using wooden spoon as stethoscope). Join in play if appropriate to help her explore her feelings about her sister being in hospital.
- Observe Tariq to see how he is negotiating for a turn – support him in this.
- Read one-to-one stories with Raj and Karen who find group story time difficult.

Obviously, it is not possible for plans to be made for every child every day. Teachers need to prioritize and decide which children need specific adult support, and which children will be able to extend their own activity if additional resources are made available. Notes such as those above serve to focus the attention of teachers and nursery nurses on specific learning needs, and to remind all staff of particular interests. Members of staff involved in implementing any of the above plans would be responsible for noting what happened.

2. *Plans for small groups of children.* This aspect of planning involves the experiences and activities which team members initiate and offer to small groups of children. Sometimes any child can opt for the activity or experience, and several small groups may be involved during the course of a session, while on other occasions adults will decide which children can take part to ensure that equality of access is achieved. These experiences may be led by parent helpers and students as well as by basic team members, and might include:

- Cooking.
- Outings into the local neighbourhood.
- Setting up an interesting display based on a recent experience or event.

- Activities to introduce or reinforce specific concepts, such as floating and sinking, turntaking, size, magnetism.
- A woodwork project, such as making a run for the class pet.
- The introduction of a new piece of equipment.
- Planting some bulbs in tubs in the outside area.
- Sewing.
- Music and movement sessions.
- Planned, as opposed to spontaneous, story sessions.

In planning these experiences, nursery teachers are increasingly recognizing the need to record:

- Why they are being offered – how they relate to the children's needs and interests.
- Which children would benefit most from being involved.
- What resources will be needed.
- What their intentions are for children's learning – which attitudes, skills and knowledge it is intended that the children might develop through their involvement in this experience.

Learning intentions have to incorporate the range of needs within the class so that the experience offers an opportunity for learning to all children who take part. If, for example, a gardening activity is planned, it should be possible for some children to handle and dig in the earth and discuss their discoveries, alongside others who are keen to learn more about planting and growing vegetables. Similarly, during a cooking activity teachers will intend that some children will benefit most from the sensory experiences involved in mixing ingredients, while for other more experienced children an intention might be to encourage them to put the changes they observe during the mixing and cooking process into words.

This does not mean that the teacher has rigid intentions for particular children. She uses her knowledge of children and her awareness of the next challenge for them to predict possible learning outcomes. However, through having a variety of possibilities in mind she is able to respond to the unexpected – the experienced child who is gaining comfort from stirring his ingredients as he tells her of a distressing experience which is worrying him (the learning outcome is still language related but not in the way the teacher expected), or the new child who exclaims as she mixes margarine and sugar 'Look! My mixture's gone lighter.'

When planning small group activities teachers must also ensure that plans are made for adult involvement in all areas of experience, and that the adults involved are aware of the possibilities for cross-curricular learning in every experience. Children are given powerful messages about male and female roles when observing adults in the nursery. Nursery staff are predominantly female, and it is easy for them to reinforce stereotypes through their own involvement in traditionally female activities such as art, cooking and sewing, and through their encouragement of male visitors to undertake activities such as woodwork or outdoor activity.

Many teachers are currently confronting these stereotypes by involving themselves in the full range of experiences, and by specifically asking fathers to bath their baby or cook in the nursery, and mothers to garden or mend wooden toys. They have had to encourage some parents to involve themselves in this way since attitudes about what men and women should do are still entrenched. This will be explored further in Chapter 5.

3. *Plans for spontaneous adult involvement.* As well as setting up and leading specific experiences for the children, adults in the nursery class also involve themselves in children's spontaneous play activities. Often this happens on the spur of the moment, but the point was made earlier that this spontaneous involvement may be fleeting and lack depth. Another problem with a reactive approach is that it has a tendency to involve some children and some areas of experience at the expense of others.

These problems may be overcome, at least to some extent, through planning loosely how adult time will be spent. Teachers and nursery nurses usually work to a rota showing which area of the nursery they will be working in at different times of the day. Each day they will spend some time out of doors and some time indoors. When involving additional adults, such as parents and students, staff need to decide where this extra help is most needed and communicate this to the person concerned.

Careful planning of the deployment of adults in the nursery is essential for effective time management. Teachers know that there are never going to be enough hours in the day, and that they will never have as many adults available as they think they need. They also know that through their planning they can ensure that time is not wasted unnecessarily, and that all available adults work to good effect.

If in-depth interactions and observations are to be undertaken and sustained, staff need to know that at certain times of the day they will be free from the daily chores, such as intervening in quarrels, changing wet pants and so on, which often cause interruptions. Clearly, it is only possible to minimize disruption if staffing ratios are favourable. In classes with one teacher and one nursery nurse (one working inside and one outside), other adults need to be added to the team on a regular basis to provide the required flexibility, while in classes with three or more members of staff it is possible for one member to take responsibility for all interruptions, while another involves herself in depth with children's play. These roles must be interchangeable, so that everyone gains experience of both kinds of work, which are equally important to the running of the nursery class and to the children's development.

In order to plan for their involvement in children's self-initiated activity, adults need to take into account their recent observations. One member of staff may, for example, have been observing a small group using some planks, milk crates and tyres to make themselves an obstacle course, when time ran out and the equipment had to be packed away. She may decide, because she is working outside the next morning, to see if they continue this play and, if so, may plan to involve herself and help them set themselves even greater challenges. Similarly, a member of staff may have observed that the brick area is being dominated by a particular group of boys and may decide to place herself in this area to encourage the boys to allow others to join in and to encourage some of the girls, who like to be near her, to take part in brick play. Or a member of staff may have observed a worrying change in one child's behaviour and may plan to observe the child again and perhaps involve herself in the child's activity with a view to finding out what is wrong.

If staff and helpers are to work as a team and not as a collection of individuals, it is essential that they share their intentions with each other so that priorities can be identified and appropriate support offered. There is nothing more frustrating than to find that you are just gaining a child's confidence, when an incident across the room takes away your attention. Sometimes this is the reality of nursery education, but it need not always be – particularly if extra adult support is encouraged.

The key to successful intervention in children's activities is observation. Without it adults run the risk of interrupting children and destroying their activity. If we want to be involved in child-initiated activity, we must watch, listen and, on the basis of what we have seen and heard, find a role for ourselves which emphasizes our status as equal partner in play and not leader of it. This aspect of the nursery teacher's role will be explored further in Chapter 5.

4. *Plans for special events*. Plans need to take into account all out-of-the ordinary occurrences. These include events such as the admission of new children, a new member of staff, a parent coming to do a baby bathing session, an informal visit by the school dentist or the fire engine, an outing by a small group of children, parents and staff to a local place of interest, a visiting theatre or puppet group, or a visit by school governors.

All members of the team including the children need to know in advance the purpose of the event, what will happen, and how they will be affected. Careful planning of special events is essential if they are not to be stressful or a complete waste of time.

Planning, both long and short term, involves a process of informed guess-work. Teachers have to identify what might capture the interest of individual children or groups of children, and work out the range of possible ways of developing this interest further. They use their knowledge of young children and their curricular knowledge to help them work through this process. Plans need to be flexible and sometimes (as we will see later in this chapter) have to be abandoned.

Recording short-term plans

Weekly or daily planning records are the working documents of the nursery team. It is unfortunate, therefore, that some teachers seem to believe that they have to be neat and tidy – that they are there more for the scrutiny of others than to inform their own practice.

This attitude is changing and it is increasingly common to see tentative, weekly forecasts of what might be offered being added to as the week progresses. By the end of the week, there is nothing neat about the plans and this is how it should be. Better this than a neat timetable which is used by no one or which is used inflexibly. Above all, planning records should demonstrate that nursery teams are thinking about children, and about their work.

Many nursery teachers use a variety of methods to record their short-term plans. These include:

- Timetabled rotas for staff indicating in which areas of the nursery they will be working at different times of the day and including any special areas of responsibility associated with setting up or tidying away. Some teams have identified the daily and weekly maintenance tasks, such as checking and repairing or replenishing resources, which have to be carried out and allocate responsibility for these on a daily or weekly basis.
- Grids with sections down the side of the page showing all areas of experience, e.g. sand, home corner, graphics area and art workshop, and the days of the week across the top – these would be used to record additional resources (with reasons for each addition) in each area of provision; specific activities to be initiated by an adult for individuals and for small groups of children; other planned adult involvement; and special events.

- Rough webs showing how particular experiences on offer that week might be developed to include all curriculum areas. For example, a teacher might plan to introduce a new musical instrument and would want to demonstrate how language and literacy, science, maths, technology, history, geography, personal and social development, art and movement (as well as, more obviously, music) could be explored from this starting point. To these rough webs she might add book titles and any other resources she may wish to have available to support and extend the children's developing interest.
- Daily notes (either in a note book or on pages to be placed in a loose-leaf folder) outlining briefly the main points from the team's informal discussions, highlighting children or activities which particularly need attention, and making clear the roles which each staff member is expected to play.

Through the written planning records the teacher reminds the team of their collective expectations, and broadens their awareness of learning possibilities. These records provide a flexible framework and are discussed and added to regularly throughout the week. They are used to evaluate the effectiveness of the provision and, clearly, the more detailed they are the more useful they will be.

Implementing Plans and Monitoring What Actually Happens

Throughout the last section on curriculum planning the need to see plans as tentative documents has been emphasized. Sometimes the experiences we provide for young children capture their interest and develop in the ways we had predicted. Sometimes they even learn what we intended them to learn. On other occasions, however, children surprise us and respond in a way which we had not predicted. This is why, when we put our plans into practice, it is essential that we monitor how the children actually respond to the provision we make, and to our interactions with them.

Clearly, it is futile for any teacher to continue to pursue her exploration of the capacity of different containers, when the learner she is working with is pre-occupied with her weekend visit to granny, which involved travelling by train for the first time. Better to talk about the visit first and then see if interest in the capacity activity develops. Even if it does not, the teacher will still have involved the child in an important learning experience. In describing to her teacher an event, which only she knows about, the child is involved in a complex intellectual and linguistic exercise. She will be motivated to persist because she wants to communicate.

Early years teachers have the advantage that young children let them know when they have been switched off, or when they are interested in something else. Unfortunately, not all teachers are able to adapt their approach in response to the messages children give (Bennett and Kell, 1989; NFER/SCDC, 1987), and as children get older they learn to keep their thoughts to themselves, and can appear to be concentrating, while in fact their thoughts are elsewhere. By the time we are adults we are expert at this kind of deception. How many of us have sat apparently engrossed at a lecture thinking about what we were going to do at the weekend?

Sharing power with children requires us to encourage them to continue to give this feedback on the curriculum we offer them, and to value their own interests and concerns. Children give feedback in a number of ways either verbally or through their actions. If we listen carefully to their responses to our suggestions or comments, and observe how they use materials or behave in the presence of adults or other children, we will gain insight into their interests and needs.

To get this kind of feedback teams need to monitor:

- The use of the learning environment. Has the space been organized effectively? Are all children gaining access to all areas of experience or are some areas being dominated? Are the learning experiences offered out of doors as varied and as rich as those on offer in the classroom? What is working well/not so well? What is missing?
- The use of equipment and materials, particularly noticing unexpected uses (the plastic pegs being stirred in the home corner saucepan indicating a need for some materials to represent food); any gaps in provision (the child searching in vain for a piece of 'fur' to make a collage cat); and any creative combinations of equipment (the small group using some woodshavings and twigs from the art workshop to complete the 'fire' in the fireplace they have built out of large, hollow blocks).
- The responses of individual children:
  - to the same adult-initiated experience – highlighting what each child did, said, and was interested in;
  - to adult involvement in their play or behaviour. How did the child respond? Did adult involvement enhance or destroy play/reinforce or change behaviour? Why?

The answers to these questions, although sometimes painful to accept, broaden the team's thinking about the provision they are making and about their own role in children's learning. It is, after all, very important to know that a child's aggressive behaviour is being reinforced by the staff's handling of her.

Chapter 5 explores further how the teacher, through her actions and interactions, puts her intentions into practice, and how she needs to adapt her plans according to children's responses.

Monitoring methods

Teams employ a variety of methods, initiated by the teacher, to help them monitor what is actually happening in their classes. They may record for a day (or over several days) on a grid which children and adults are working in each area of experience at 15- or 30-minute intervals, in order to highlight which areas of provision might be being dominated, which are not being used, or are being neglected by the adults, which are overcrowded, and so on. This general view might be followed up by team discussion, and more focused observations to gain a more detailed view.

All members of the team, including student and parent helpers, are encouraged by the teacher to jot down in a small notebook which they all keep with them, any interesting uses of equipment, or responses by individual children to activities or adult intervention. These are discussed informally at the end of each day or before school starts in the morning, and used to initiate specific observations (to find out more about particular children) or to inform future planning. Those adults who are not confident to write can be encouraged to contribute their observations verbally.

Teachers will also ask regular visitors to the class, such as the headteacher, adviser, governors and, of course, parents, for their perceptions of how the class is actually working. They may also call in specialists, such as educational psychologists, to help them gain an outsider's view of what is happening – particularly in relation to behavioural difficulties.

These more objective views are important because often staff are too closely involved to see clearly what is at the root of a situation. One team were surprised to discover, when asking an educational psychologist to observe a child who was causing them concern, that, after a morning spent observing, she expressed more concern for the child's friend, who was acting in a subtly manipulative way, and was responsible for some of her friend's extreme behaviour. The team, which had been stretched to the limit dealing with this extreme behaviour, had failed to see one of the underlying causes, and were extremely grateful for this challenge to their assumptions.

The Open University (1981, p. 234) suggest six questions to help teachers learn more about the received curriculum:

1. What did the pupils actually do?
2. What were they learning?

3. How worthwhile was it?
4. What did I do?
5. What did I learn?
6. What do I intend to do now?

The extent to which nursery staff are prepared to ask themselves these questions will determine the quality of the curriculum they offer and the relevance of this curriculum to the children they work with.

Identifying Achievements and Reviewing Progress

'What children can do, not what they cannot do, is the starting point in children's education' (EYCG, 1989, p. 3). An understanding of this principle of early childhood education has never been more important, since many nursery age children are currently being educated in reception classes where they are being given tasks they could not be expected to do (Bennett and Kell, 1989).

Teachers of young children must find ways of establishing what each child knows and can do, and use this information to identify starting points which offer each child a chance of success. The child who has managed to do a four piece shape inset puzzle would clearly have little chance of success if she is given, or chooses, a twelve piece interlocking jigsaw to put together. She might be successful, though, if she were helped to select a five- or six-piece inset tray straight after completing the four-piece puzzle – particularly if she was offered support by an adult.

In order to make these kinds of judgements, teachers have to add to the knowledge of each child which they gained from parents and other under-5s' workers, by observing the child's achievements in the school context. If each child is to be treated equally, teams know that they must develop a system which ensures that all children are regularly the focus of attention, and that the progress of all children is reviewed from time to time. Earlier in this chapter, the kinds of methods used to record children's achievements and progress were outlined. In this section, we focus on the kinds of information teachers record.

Most of the information collected by team members is in the form of written or verbally communicated observations. Unless these are focused and organized in some way, they can become repetitive, and it is often difficult to extract relevant information from them. In reviewing the strengths and weaknesses of their recordkeeping systems, teachers have recognized the need to help their team develop a set of guidelines outlining the kinds of information it is useful to record.

Using published materials, their own policy statements, and, most recently, the National Curriculum documents, each team will develop their own guidelines. Most teachers agree that records should be positive, and should provide evidence of what children have achieved, so that they can be used to make plans to enable the child to consolidate his learning, and progress to the next stage. However, they also recognize that it will only be possible to give appropriate support if any concerns about the child's development are identified.

The kinds of information teams might record include the following:

- Attendance record – the regularity of attendance, punctuality and the effects of these on school achievement. Nursery education is non-statutory and occasionally parents do not see the need to take their child regularly or on time. If staff can provide evidence that the child's achievements and relationships are negatively affected by irregular attendance patterns, the situation usually improves quickly.
- Relationships – with peers and adults including particular friendships; sharing, turntaking and negotiating ability; understanding of rules; his or her ability to care for and empathize with others, etc.
- Feelings – the child's ability to express feelings and control them when appropriate; any worries or anxieties.
- Confidence and self-esteem (as exhibited in school) – situations in which the child is most/least confident; his or her ability to be assertive and stand up for his or her own rights or ask an adult for support.
- Independence – self-help skills, e.g. toileting, feeding and dressing; his or her ability to use the whole nursery environment, select resources, plan his or her own time, ask for support when required; his or her ability to take responsibility for clearing up, for younger children, taking messages, etc.
- Preferred activities – how a child chooses to spend time in the nursery, i.e. which activities and how they are used.
- Physical growth – the child's ability to use nursery equipment (climbing frames, bats and balls, see-saws, bikes, etc.); body control (running, jumping, hopping, skipping, kicking, throwing, etc.); use of tools (for drawing, painting, cutting, woodwork, sewing, cooking, etc.), and other equipment (for building, threading, doll dressing, etc.).
- Attitude to learning – motivation; curiosity; use of imagination; his or her ability to cope with and learn from problems or failure; persistence; his or her ability to respond to new experiences.

Nursery teams also record achievements within subject areas:

- English – speaking and listening – his or her ability to:
  - express needs,
  - describe present and past experiences,
  - ask questions,
  - describe a sequence of events,
  - reason and supply logical explanations,
  - talk imaginatively,
  - retell or make up stories in their own words,
  - explain a process,
  - take a message,
  - negotiate verbally.

  It is important that bilingual children are assessed in the language used at home as well as English to give a full view of a child's linguistic competence.
- English – reading and writing:
  - response to story times,
  - interest in books (story and reference),
  - ability to handle books appropriately,
  - ability to recognize that words tell stories,
  - interest in written words,
  - interest in his or her own talk written down by an adult,
  - interest in reading his or her own talk written down,
  - ability to read names or words in books,
  - interest in letters and sounds,
  - interest in writing,
  - ability to write name or other words.
- Mathematics – his or her ability to:
  - sort objects or materials in the course of play or tidying up and explain reasons for groupings,
  - make comparisons, e.g. height, weight, size, texture, etc.,
  - use the language of position – between, over, under, inside, outside, on, behind, in front, etc.,
  - put graded objects into order, e.g. graded saucepans, beakers, cubes, etc., in the course of play and use the language of size, e.g. big, bigger, biggest,
  - construct with 2-D and 3-D shapes and name and describe properties of some regular shapes,
  - use numbers – count in one-to-one correspondence in the course of play, e.g. one plate for each doll; carry out simple addition and subtraction, e.g. if you take one cake there will be two left; recognize numbers in the environment,

- put events into time sequence – knowing what happens next during the nursery day,
- make patterns in a variety of situations and discuss patterns in the environment.
- Science – his or her ability to:
  - make and discuss observations of everyday objects, materials, living creatures and plantlife,
  - question their experiences and plan and set up their own explorations,
  - communicate their discoveries to others,
  - make predictions to suggest what would happen if. . .,
  - interpret the results of their explorations, e.g. this boat floats because it's made of wood,
  - tackle and find a solution to problems.

  In addition to achievements under the above headings, which are concerned with the scientific process, nursery teachers increasingly need to record experiences children have gained which are relevant to the specific content of the National Curriculum document on science, e.g. experience of types and uses of materials, forces, electricity and processes of life.
- Technology – his or her experience of:
  - the use and effects of tools,
  - the exploration of properties and use of materials,
  - the exploration of design features,
  - the uses of technology in the environment,
  - the use of tools and materials to design and make models, including their planning and problem solving ability,
  - design features, e.g. when examining component parts of a clock or telephone which has been taken apart, or when looking at buildings in the local environment,
  - the use of a computer, tape recorder and simple camera.
- Aesthetic and creative – his or her
  - interest in activities such as drawing, painting, woodwork, modelling, clay, music, movement and drama,
  - ability to represent ideas using a variety of media,
  - use of imagination,
  - use of tools and materials,
  - stage of drawing and painting development.

When reviewing the child's achievements, areas where encouragement or specific help – either because of an exceptional aptitude or because of a lack of confidence or developmental delay – are noted.

One major problem faced by teachers when they try to summarize a child's achievements is how to extract the specific information they need from their collection of observations. Some are now considering ways of coding observations (particularly the more detailed focused observations), and the dated work samples they collect, to highlight the kinds of evidence they contain.

If we consider the following observation:

> Samantha (4 yrs 1 mth) sat down at the dough table and asked Ahmed if she could have a piece of dough. He gave her a small piece and she said: 'That's not much. You've got a big lot and I've only got this tiny bit. Can I have some more please.' She helped Ahmed to share out the dough so they had roughly pieces of equal size. She then selected from the shelves a cake tin with spaces for nine cakes, a rolling pin and a cutter. She matched the cutters against the holes in the cake tin and chose the one closest in size to the holes. She then rolled out the dough and began to cut out the cakes placing them into the tin one at a time. She commented to the nursery teacher 'The tin's nearly full.' The nursery teacher replied: 'Yes it is. How many more cakes do you think you need to cut?' She glanced at the tray and answered correctly 'Three more'. She finished filling the tray and placed it into the toy cooker next to the dough table turning the control knobs as she did so. She then said to the nursery nurse 'I'm going shopping now. Can you look after my cakes please.'

We can see that it provides information relevant to the following headings – relationships (negotiating with Ahmed); confidence (in use of resources); independence (planning her own activity and selecting from a range of equipment); physical skills (use of tools); attitude to learning (persistence in seeing her activity through to its conclusion); English: speaking and listening (when reasoning with Ahmed); and mathematics (when choosing the right size cutter and when working out how many more cakes she needed to cut). This is true of most observations.

By devising a coding system, based perhaps on the first letters of the headings in their own guidelines, teachers can mark their observations so that they can see at a glance where they will find evidence of particular aspects of a child's learning. When they go through the section for a particular child in the observation file or index box, they can see more easily what kinds of evidence are missing and can plan with their team how to gain additional information.

Developing a system for reviewing children's progress

If teachers want to ensure that all children make progress, they need to devise a system which focuses their attention on each child's achievements at particular points in time. The profile completed before children start at nursery provides the team with a starting point. They will want to complete a further profile to show the child's response to the school experience during his or her first term (but not before the child has adjusted to the new setting), and will be required to complete a transfer record when the child leaves the nursery class to go to infant school. Between these two school profiles or records, teachers will review each child's progress as often as possible. The frequency with which they are able to do this will depend largely on the numbers of children in the class and on the staffing situation. During periods of staff absence it is always difficult to keep systems going.

Some teams now regularly (perhaps once a term) complete a form for each child summarizing a child's achievements under headings similar to those in the previous section. In order to do this, they select a number of children (how many depends on the situation) each week for all team members to focus on. Often the teacher will have checked the existing records for these children to discover the kinds of information the team have already collected, and that which they need to look out for during the week. At the end of the week an opportunity is made for the team to discuss their observations and complete a profile.

Formalizing recordkeeping in this way ensures that no child is missed, and that children who are not making progress, and may have special educational needs, are identified.

Sharing Perceptions with Others and Identifying Needs

The records described in this chapter are informed by, and offer a focus for, communication between nursery staff, parents and other professionals. Teachers and nursery nurses consider the informal discussions they engage in daily to be a vital part of their work. These daily interactions help keep all staff up to date with the most recent developments, and foster a mutual commitment to their work and to the children.

Teams also see the importance of making time for more focused, in-depth discussions about aspects of policy and practice and about the children, and often organize weekly meetings for this purpose. These meetings are usually set up for specific purposes – either to discuss a practice issue, such as the ordering of new equipment, or to review some of the children. An expected outcome of these meetings will be a collective identification of needs (both in relation to policy and practice development and to children's development) based on information supplied by all members of the team. Sometimes the team will involve other professionals, such as speech therapists, concerned with a child in sharing their perceptions. In this way, a consistent approach is more likely to be achieved.

Some teachers offer parents opportunities to share their view of their child's experience at home and at school. A natural extension of the pre-school profile has been the regular involvement of parents in recordkeeping. Teachers have realized that, in addition to their informal daily chats with parents, both they and parents would benefit greatly from meeting together more formally to discuss children's progress.

Using achievement profiles completed by the nursery staff as an introduction to the discussion, teachers invite parents (with an interpreter if necessary) to add their views about their child's achievements, particularly the developments and interests they have noticed at home. These discussions also provide an opportunity for parents to question what happens in nursery class, and for teachers to learn about the child in the home situation. In this way, parents and staff can work together in the interests of the child.

Making More Plans

The recordkeeping process has now come full circle. Information is collected, plans are made and implemented, more information is collected, and plans are reviewed in the light of evidence contributed by all team members. It is now time to plan again.

Through sharing their perceptions of what actually took place and what children did and have achieved, the nursery team can decide what further action they need to take. At the end of a meeting with parents, plans to extend a particular child's learning at home and school can be made. Having identified the child's achievements so far, staff and parents can decide what kinds of experiences and adult support are necessary to ensure that progress continues.

This process of finding out, using information to make plans, monitoring plans in action, and sharing perceptions, lies at the heart of the responsive nursery curriculum. Nursery records in the past were sometimes little more than meaningless pieces of paper which were rarely used in meaningful ways. In trying to develop methods which more closely match their purposes and intentions, teachers have been intensely challenged. They freely admit there is much more to be done, and yet the most effective teachers have a great deal to be proud of. HMI (DES, 1989a, p. 5), in highlighting the quality of the education received by children attending nursery schools and classes, comment 'The work is well planned with a suitable emphasis on purposeful play and exploratory activity'. Purposeful planning can only occur if records of the kind outlined above are made a priority. A plea for the time needed to undertake this work is made in the final chapter.

Some Points for Discussion

Evaluating Existing Records

Collect all the written documents you have produced for your class. To what extent do they communicate to the team and to others:

- Your aims for all aspects of your work? (For example, the curriculum, equal opportunities, health and safety, settling children into the nursery, and parental involvement.)
- How you intend to put these aims into practice? (For example, policy statements and curriculum planning.)

Think about the records you keep to provide evidence of children's achievements in your class. Consider the oldest group in your present class, i.e. those transferring shortly to the reception class: which of these children do you know most/least well? (One way of approaching this is to make a list from memory of these children – which ones came to mind first/last or not at all?) Identify one or two children you feel you know well, and one or two you feel you know less well. Collect all the recorded information you have on these children, examine it carefully and ask yourself: what does this tell you about the strengths and weaknesses of your current approach to assessment?

Improving Recordkeeping

The questions addressed in this chapter are ones which all teachers need to consider in relation to their own practice. It is essential to ask:

- Why keep records? What are my purposes? What kind of records would match my purposes?
- What information should records contain? What information do I and others need? What information is it most useful to collect?
- Who should contribute to the records and for what purpose? How can various contributions be co-ordinated?
- Which are the best ways of recording different kinds of information?
- What use is to be made of the information which has been collected? If the answer is 'no use', then what is the point of keeping the information?
- How will I review my recordkeeping system to ensure that it is manageable, relevant and useful?

Observation as an Integral Part of Recordkeeping

To what extent is observation encouraged in your class? For what purposes? How could you ensure that all team members regularly make time to observe? What do you feel it is important to observe? Make a list of the kinds of situations you want to observe objectively. (For example, a new child during her first few days, a new piece of equipment in use, a child working in a group, a new or reorganized area of experience.) Ask yourself:

- How can you make relatively uninterrupted time for observation? (Think about those things which prevent you from observing and consider how you could overcome these difficulties.)
- Which methods of recording will you use? (Laishley (1987) suggests a number of alternative methods.)
- How will you share and make use of the observations made by all team members?

Which parts of the recordkeeping process described in this chapter do you feel you need/would like to develop? What support will you need to develop your work in the ways you have identified? How will you make a case to get this support?

5

THE NURSERY TEACHER AS ENABLER AND PLAYMATE

The role of play and talk in children's learning, and the need for teachers to develop a responsive style of interaction, have already been emphasized. We know also that 'there is potential in all children which emerges powerfully under favourable conditions' (EYCG, 1989, p. 3). In the last chapter, we saw how teachers keep detailed records to help them discover the most favourable learning conditions for each child, and how this involves them in working in close partnership with colleagues, parents, and the children themselves.

In this chapter the personal qualities and skills required by teachers, if they are to put these ideas into practice through their interactions with the children, will be explored further. Teachers regularly face demands from those who wish to see children being 'made to' sit down and do some 'real work'. Obviously, early years educators have still not been able to communicate effectively to the general public (or even their own colleagues) their understanding of the learning process. Communication has been made more difficult by the emphasis on so-called traditional, 'back to basics' methods in recent press articles.

It would be relatively easy for teachers to give in to the demands of others. Young children, because they are usually eager to please adults, can be persuaded to do what is asked of them, however little it means to them (Katz and Chard, 1989). Donaldson (1978) points out that many children, as they grow older, become dispirited through being given tasks which are beyond their capability, or which do not interest them, and that many have given up by the time they reach adolescence. If we are to reverse this trend and maintain the confidence and enthusiasm which children demonstrate in the early years, it is essential that nursery teachers retain their principles, and that primary and secondary teachers learn from the approaches of their nursery colleagues. There are signs that they are already doing so – after all, what is the GCSE examination if not an extension of good, early years practice? The principles of early childhood education can and should be applied to learning at all stages.

The Teacher's Aims for Children's Learning

It may be that some readers have formed the impression that children attending nursery class can do as they like, and only learn what they choose to learn. This is certainly a misconception held by some casual visitors to nursery classes – particularly by those who believe learning only takes place as a result of formal instruction. It is therefore important to expand on the previous chapters and summarize the role of the teacher in influencing the content of the curriculum for individual children.

Katz and Chard (1989) provide a helpful overview of the kinds of goals teachers need to have for children's learning. They identify four major types of learning goal: 'knowledge, skills, dispositions, and feelings' (p. 20). In common with teachers of older children, nursery teachers want children to acquire knowledge (concepts, ideas, facts, etc.) and skills, such as cutting with scissors, recognizing and writing their name, and throwing a ball accurately. The awareness of all teachers of the range of knowledge and skills children should be exposed to has been heightened by the introduction of the National Curriculum. Although the under-5s are not included within the National Curriculum framework, teachers have been keen to demonstrate the relevance of the experience children gain in the nursery class to the programmes of study, and to record evidence of attainment as appropriate (EYCG, 1989; Lally, 1989a).

This is not to imply that teachers are now taking their lead from the National Curriculum. Their starting point is still the children, but they also recognize the need to make themselves aware of educational developments, and the need to encourage primary colleagues and parents to value the experiences they offer nursery age children as a foundation (rather than as preparation) for later learning. They would be failing in their duty if they did not inform infant teachers of the children's achievements in the nursery class.

However, the aquisition of knowledge and skills, although important, is not the only concern of the nursery teacher. She knows that young children will be more likely to acquire knowledge and skills if she also encourages them to develop positive dispositions and feelings. Katz and Chard (1989, pp. 20–1) define dispositions as 'habits of mind, or tendencies to respond to situations in characteristic ways'. Persistence, curiosity, initiative and interest are all examples of dispositions. There is evidence that an over-concentration on skills and knowledge aquisition at the expense of dispositions is counterproductive in the long term (Schweinhart, Weikart and Larner, 1986) – after all, what is the point in having skills if you do not have the disposition to make use of them? Many adults never read for pleasure even though they can read. This is because they learnt the skills involved in reading, but were not helped to acquire the disposition to read. Nursery teachers aim to build on the children's natural curiosity and zest for life and encourage an enthusiasm for learning.

In Chapter 2 the role of the teacher in helping children to feel confident, accepted, competent and powerful was described. Ensuring that all children develop and retain these feelings in the school situation should be a primary concern for all teachers. Nursery teachers have a particular responsibility to foster this development, because they are involved with the child's first contact with school. Many teachers express the hope that the dispositions and feelings which children have acquired in their class will stay with them through life, and will help them to cope with the less favourable conditions they might meet in the future.

In this chapter we will see how nursery teachers support and influence children's experiences with all these goals in mind. Because they are concerned with the development of dispositions and feelings, they do not make children sit down to learn a particular skill – they know that this would be likely to lead to resentment and, possibly, to feelings of incompetence. Moreover, they are well aware that there are many opportunities for introducing skills and knowledge during activities the children have chosen for themselves from the carefully structured provision, and that sensitive adult intervention in these activities is more likely to result in the desired learning outcome.

Responsive Teaching – What is Involved?

The role of the teacher as described so far has emphasized the need to lead the team in creating an inspiring learning environment, observing how children make use of it, and adapting the provision and adult involvement in response to children's interests and needs. Responsive teaching of this kind is only possible if the adults involved have developed a range of personal qualities.

The point has already been made that teachers act as role models for the children – it is no coincidence that teachers with loud voices produce classes of noisy children, and that teachers who use negotiating strategies produce children who can negotiate with each other! However, it is not just behaviour which is imitated. If teachers wish to encourage the acquisition of knowledge, skills, dispositions and feelings, they need to have acquired these themselves in order to be able to demonstrate their value.

Nursery teachers need:

- *Knowledge:* of child development, of the backgrounds and experience of individual children, and of subject content (in order to be able to recognize opportunities for introducing facts or concepts).
- *Skills:* including communication skills, some practical skills (which develop through the pursuit of personal interests in art, gardening, music, woodwork, pottery, cookery, scientific exploration, writing, etc.), and organizational skills.
- *Dispositions:* similar to those they expect children to develop such as an inquiring mind, curiosity, interest, warmth, persistence and a willingness to have a go.
- *Feelings*, such as confidence, enthusiasm and pleasure in the achievements of others.

Just as with children, knowledge and skills alone are not enough. A government White Paper (DES, 1983, 1.26) states 'Personality, character and commitment are as important as the specific knowledge and skills that are used in the day to day tasks of teaching'. Some of the most academically able teachers fail dismally to engage the children, because they are unable to demonstrate or encourage appropriate dispositions and feelings alongside the academic content of their teaching. The way many of these teachers were taught themselves was not conducive to the development of anything other than raw facts or isolated skills – how many of us learnt about magnetism from the teacher's diagrams on the blackboard without ever touching a magnet? If they were not encouraged to apply their learning in real life situations, it is inevitably going to be difficult for them to help children do this.

Learning how to Learn

Many teachers talk about the joy of learning how to learn for the first time when they start to observe and work alongside nursery children. This joy is unlikely to be felt by those who have not been supported by appropriate training, because these teachers are usually unable to make sense of what they see and hear young children doing and saying, and are not expecting children to teach them anything.

A secondary trained teacher, who had returned to teaching after a career break and had been placed in a nursery school without the benefit of any retraining, commented to her colleagues that she thought the nursery must be very boring for the children. She felt that, because the staff had created a learning environment where everything had a definite place and where children could operate autonomously, children would get bored because the rooms always looked essentially the same. Of course, this view took no account of the fact that the experienced staff adapted the learning environment in subtle ways in response to their observations, or of the fact that children were using this environment very confidently and with ever developing competence. A colleague asked her: 'Do you think the children look bored?' After thinking for a moment she said 'No, they always look very busy and involved. But I would be bored if I was them.' This was what was at the root of her comment – she was bored because she did not know how to relate to children who were operating so independently of her. She felt she and the rest of the staff ought to be initiating lots of exciting activities for the children to do – in this way she could feel she had a role and that the children needed her (in a very dependent way, of course).

This example highlights a dilemma which many nursery staff have faced when translating principles, and messages from research into practice. Many adults, particularly those who have been used to directing activities, have found that giving children more power and control over their learning has involved them in rethinking their whole approach. Some briefly (or not so briefly in some cases) found it difficult to relinquish power over children and some felt they no longer had a role to play. With the benefit of experience, teams have learnt from children that adult support is still necessary, and that a less didactic model of support actually has more potential in terms of lasting learning. In-service training opportunities have been essential to help teachers and nursery nurses develop these alternative strategies, and to support each other through the upheavals which change inevitably brings with it.

For many teachers, the changes have been exciting ones. These teachers have been delighted to observe the progress children can make in a less restricted setting. They have seen for themselves that their own expectations have a powerful influence on children's achievements and, above all, they have been inspired by the children to engage in experiences they would never have tried alone, such as allowing a centipede to crawl across your hand to protect it from their enthusiasm, or responding to their excited requests for you to sit on the police horse just like they did.

A transmission model of teaching is relatively safe for the teacher as she is in control, and can initiate or put a stop to activities as the mood takes her. This approach also very quickly becomes boring because it closes the teacher off from the learners' ideas.

A responsive approach to children feels much less safe for the teacher, because children share control and have an equal right to initiate or end activities. Teachers cannot be sure where the learners will lead them, or that they will follow the leads the teacher introduces. This approach is never boring though. It offers both teachers and pupils the chance to learn from each other and is all the richer for that. It requires teachers to make countless judgements and adjustments during the course of each day – an intellectually demanding process.

In order to adopt this approach, nursery staff have to accept the role of learner, and have to replace the role of director of learning (which implies a hierarchical structure), with the roles of enabler and playmate (which emphasize a partnership approach to learning). There is certainly nothing easy about this method of teaching.

Personal Characteristics of the Teacher

Some in-service trainers put teachers into rooms full of the kinds of materials and equipment to be found in the early years classroom and ask them to explore. It is fascinating to observe how teachers respond to this opportunity, and it is from these observations that it is possible to gain clues about the personal characteristics required by the teacher.

Three main responses can usually be observed. First there are the writers. These teachers have arrived with notebooks and are determined to use them. They spend the entire session walking round the room noting book titles, listing equipment and asking about stockists. They do not use any of the equipment, they merely pick up some items to look at them more closely. Second are the embarrassed watchers. These teachers move around the room stopping at each activity or piece of equipment, and handling something in an embarrassed way without any purpose. While doing this they watch (out of the corner of their eye) what others are doing. Third are the enthusiastic players. They have a good look round to begin with (often with a friend) and then decide what they will do. They spend the whole session playing at one or two activities, finding out how things work, setting themselves problems to solve, and sometimes being naughty – often with water.

These descriptions are obviously stereotypical. Perhaps they are unkind. They are not intended to be. They have been included to remind us how our response to situations can give us insight into our own attitude to learning. Most teachers can probably relate to all three types, since all of us find it easier to get involved with some activities than others. It does not need spelling out which of the three types of teacher would be most likely to inspire and respond effectively to the children in her class.

It is a sad fact that many of us have suppressed the playful side of our personality. Without it we are unlikely to be able to empathize with young children's playful responses. If, for example, we have forgotten how much fun it can be to be naughty or to play a trick on someone, we are likely to deal much too harshly with children's experiments with the boundaries of acceptable behaviour. After all, blowing water through a tube is irresistible, so how can you be expected to stop just because it is landing on someone's head? If we want children to take responsibility for their actions, we must allow them to consider and discuss calmly the consequences of their actions.

An ability to enjoy, and to share in the enjoyment of others, is an essential characteristic for the teacher. So is an ability to see the world through a child's eyes. Without these abilities we are unlikely to be spontaneously invited to share in children's adventures – they are hardly likely to ask us to get involved if they know we will put a dampener on their pursuits. Teachers who feel they have lost these abilities can quickly recapture them if they allow children to help them. Allowing children to help requires us to let go of our adult inhibitions or at least of some of them. We must not worry about making ourselves look foolish – in the eyes of the children we do not look foolish, even if we are wearing a hat from the dressing up box.

Of course, enjoyment is not the only aim of nursery education, although it is a 'side effect or by-product of being engaged in worthwhile activity, effort and learning' (Katz and Chard, 1989, p. 5). Teachers also need to know when to be solemn and to take their pupils concerns seriously. Many of the young child's perceptions of the world seem funny to the adult. We have to remember that they are not so to the child and, that if we wish to encourage the expression of developing ideas and concepts, we must treat children with respect.

Adrian (aged 4½), who had just been baptized, was re-enacting the church service with a group of friends. He invited his teacher to join in. He had taken the role of the priest and organized his friends and the teacher to sit on chairs in a semi-circle in the book corner. He gave them each a 'prayer book' and then told them to 'sing this after me'. He began to chant solemnly 'come by liver us, come by liver us, come by liver us Lord'. As the play continued, Adrian was stretched to the limit of his intellectual and linguistic abilities to explain how he wanted his non-Catholic friends and teacher to behave. The teacher's role on this occasion was to enable him to take the lead in reconstructing an important personal experience. She entered into the solemn nature of this activity, and gave no hint that there were times when she was amused. In common with the other children, she acted the part of a member of his congregation asking for explanation when necessary. She made a point of sharing her observations of Adrian with his mother at the end of the session, because she felt his family needed this information in order to support his growing understanding of his religion.

This sensitivity to children's moods is vital. Teachers need to be able to match their own interactions to the mood of the children's activity. The teacher who regularly responds earnestly to a playful interlude, or laughs at a child's serious remark will soon find children avoiding her.

A further personal quality is warmth. This is a difficult quality to define but those on the receiving end of an interaction know whether or not they have been communicated with warmly or not. The sincere smile, the interested question or comment, the encouraging glance or remark, the sympathetic cuddle, or the firm but understanding reprimand, all demonstrate that the teacher has noticed and cares. Above all, warmth is what young children need consistently from their teachers (Isaacs, 1954). They have been cared about at home and have the right to be cared about at school. Those of us who can remember from our early schooldays how lonely it felt to feel invisible within the group, or to be continually out of favour with the teacher, will understand the importance of these signs of positive recognition. The children need to see that their parents are also responded to warmly. The most skilled teachers can adapt their approach to reach even those children and parents who seem unreachable.

In short, then, teachers need to care, to be interested and interesting (ESAC, 1989), to join in, and to be able to share in both fun and solemn pursuits. Teachers who exhibit these qualities attract children. The children want to do things with them and want to share their experiences with them. From this sound relationship teachers are in a strong position to help children develop and learn.

The Teacher as Enabler

As we have seen, children start nursery having had very different experiences. Some will be more confident than others and more able to take advantage of the opportunities for learning which are to be found in the nursery class. It is the teacher's job to broaden the horizons of all children by finding out what they already know, and taking their learning forward.

She enables each child to learn and develop the knowledge, skills, dispositions and feelings already described by helping them to sustain their current interests, and also by interesting them in new things. The role of enabler involves her in using a number of teaching roles and strategies. Sometimes she initiates experiences with a view to stimulating, supporting or extending interest. Sometimes she acts as a role model for the children to encourage particular kinds of dispositions or skills. Sometimes she demonstrates skills or imparts knowledge. Often she uses a combination of these strategies. Whichever approach she uses, she keeps the needs of the individual in mind to help her determine the optimum moment for learning – the moment when the child wants to, or needs to, learn.

Stimulating, Sustaining and Extending Interest

The first task for any teacher is to capture the children's interest and offer starting points for learning. Having captured their interest it is then equally important to sustain and extend it. Teachers employ a variety of strategies to stimulate the curiosity of individual children and groups and use this curiosity as a starting point for cross-curricular learning. These strategies include the following.

Adding equipment to particular areas

This may be done:

- *In response to observed behaviour.* In one class the children had been observed making police and fire service vehicles with the large, hollow, wooden blocks, and had been using these in dramatic play. They were using small, rectangular blocks as 'walkie talkie' radios. The teacher, remembering that she had two unwanted, broken pocket radios at home, brought these into school the next day and added them to the block play area. These added a further dimension to the play as the children learnt where the on/off switch was, how to change the frequency and how to put the aerial up and down. The teacher planned to be involved in the block area for the first part of the session so that she could support the children in learning how to share and take turns with the radios (any new item of equipment has novelty value and will be wanted by everyone), and in learning about two-way radios. She noted that a further extension would be to ask the local beat officers to call and show their radio to the children and talk about how they used it.

- *To arouse curiosity.* Resources are not always placed in an area in response to observations of the children. Teachers also judge the kinds of additions which will fascinate the children. In one nursery school, the whole staff team had been on a technology course one evening. They had been asked to make boats from junk materials, and were able to keep their creations. It was decided to put these boats on a plank across the top of the water tray the next day and to observe how the children reacted. Several children were struck by the odd sight in their water tray – it looked like a lot of junk! One child exclaimed 'What's all this?' – the cue for the teacher to explain what the staff had been involved in, to answer the children's questions about which boat belonged to which member of staff, and to ask the children who were interested to find out which boat stayed afloat longest.

When they had made their decision she asked them to explain why they thought this boat stayed afloat longest, helping them to express their discoveries in words by prompting them with questions like 'Do you think it was because this boat is small?' To which one child replied 'No, this one's smaller and it broke.' The children themselves decided to tell each member of staff what had happened to their boat and took great delight in telling one teacher 'Your boat's no good. It's all broken.' Lucy (aged 4 years) decided she wanted to make a boat and several others joined her in the art and craft workshop area where they spent the remainder of the morning making and testing boats.

Additions to equipment are not always followed up by the teacher in this way. The teacher's time is limited and for much of the time children pursue their interests with another adult, alone, or with other children – this is why the careful planning of the learning environment is so important. However, even if a teacher cannot spend time with some children because she has decided to involve herself with others, she and her team can make sure resources are available which would enable all children to develop their interests. She can ensure that the books on flight are displayed prominently to inspire the children who were trying to make paper aeroplanes this morning; she can put buckets of water and large decorating brushes near the play house so that the children can go beyond pretending to paint the walls; she can put old order forms in the graphics area to enable those children, who watched her order some equipment, to imitate what she had done; she can hang long scarves in the dressing up area to enable the little girl, who wishes to imitate her mother with the new baby, to carry a doll on her back, and so on. This kind of responsiveness relies on the teacher's knowledge and understanding of the children's individual needs.

The thoughtful teacher reviews equipment throughout each day, adding and taking away items in the light of her observations. If the required resources are not immediately available, or she is unable to respond on that day because of her involvement in other activities, she makes a note to remind herself to discuss with other members of the team how they could extend what she and they have observed.

Setting up a display or area of interest

Teachers set up displays both to inspire interest and to build on existing interest. These displays are not just for looking at. They are also for touching and talking about and are, therefore, situated where children can see and use them easily. Sometimes they develop into a role play area or inspire a specific activity.

Displays set up to inspire interest might include:

- Photographs taken on a teacher's or nursery nurse's holiday plus items collected, such as shells, rocks, fossils and souvenirs, to inspire holiday talk.
- A collection of objects which can be taken apart, such as interlocking wooden puzzles, an old radio, graded, nesting dolls or barrels and pieces from different types of constuction kit, to encourage discussion of design features and experience of taking apart and putting together.
- Pictures and examples of different kinds of fruit to encourage discussion and tasting, and to provide the focus for cooking sessions.

Often the teacher will start a display and encourage children to contribute to it, e.g. children may bring photos and items collected on their holiday for the holiday display.

More often, though, displays or areas are set up in response to an already developing interest, or to serve as a reminder of an interesting activity. Responsive displays of this kind might be:

- Set up after a visit by the school dentist. Books, posters and items left by the dentist, such as mirrors and plastic teeth, would enable staff and children to discuss the visit and any fears the children may have and would almost certainly inspire role play.
- Set up around an item brought to school by a child. Andrew (aged 3½) had been to visit relatives in Canada and had brought a hat he had worn there to show his teacher. The hat was a balaclava helmet complete with face cover with slits for eyes and nose. This item generated much interest and discussion, and led to the setting up of a collection of headwear worn

in different climates and for different purposes and also books, photographs and posters.

- Set up after an activity, such as cooking or after an outing, to serve as a reminder of the experience, and to enable those children who took part to relive their experience in words and share it with other children.

In setting up displays, teachers are aware of the need to monitor their use and relevance to the children's interests. Displays can quickly become stale and uninspiring, and then either need to be taken down or regenerated by the addition of other items. The most successful displays and areas of interest involve staff, parents and children in contributing ideas and items, and can provide a powerful link between the children's home and school experience.

Organizing outings

Further links between school and the children's community are encouraged by outings within the local area. These links are encouraged because teachers are aware that school provides a narrow learning environment which can be divorced from the real world. Through visits children, parents and teachers can discover together what the community offers in the way of starting points for learning.

Outings involving small groups of children and adults are usually considered most valuable because they provide shared experiences, and can transform a routine activity into 'a planned educational experience' (Tizard and Hughes, 1984, p. 262). These include everyday activities such as shopping, going to the post office or bank, or taking a pet to the vet, as well as trips to the fire station, a local museum, the park, or local workshops. Occasional outings to places further afield, such as the seaside, a wildlife park or a theatre performance, involving the whole class and their parents may also be arranged.

In arranging outings, staff and other adults involved will have clear intentions, and will have discussed ways of stimulating the children's interest. They will also have ideas for following the visit up at school and at home. A small group of children had been 'writing' letters to each other and pretending to post them. Their teacher arranged a visit to the local sorting office so that they could see what happened to letters once they were posted. Whilst there they posted a letter addressed to the school and watched as it was sorted – there was great excitement the next day when the letter was delivered.

Visits, if they are to result in learning, must be carefully planned

(Ironbridge Gorge Museum, 1989). The teacher had to explain to the staff in the sorting office (as well as to all adults involved in the visit) why she wanted the children to come, and what she hoped they would learn. She also needed to provide opportunities for follow-up work so that the children could consolidate their learning – she, and the children involved in the visit, set up a sorting office in the classroom using some of the resources they had been given during the visit. They also made photos taken during the outing into a book for the whole class to share. In these ways, the interest of the children involved in the visit was sustained and other children, who had not been able to go, were also drawn into the experience. Parents were told about the experience, and several of them followed it up at home by encouraging their children to send letters to relatives.

In demonstrating how a variety of everyday experiences can offer starting points for learning, teachers validate the child's home and community experience, and encourage parents to see many of the routine tasks which they and their children undertake in the context of the child's education.

Acting as a Role Model

Teachers have increasingly recognized the need for children to see adults using their skills and knowledge. If children are to develop the disposition to read, write, climb, paint, etc., they need to see that others enjoy using these skills and find them useful. Teachers can help children to see the purpose of, and become interested in, a wide range of activities if they are prepared to demonstrate their skills, and encourage other adults to use their talents in meaningful contexts. Too often adults keep their own activities hidden from children, and yet we have already seen that children learn from imitating a more experienced person. This imitation is not merely copying. Through watching others with more experience and expertise the child 'makes use of and reconstructs an event after the event' (Bruce, 1987, p. 73).

The teacher inspires an interest in reading and writing through her own involvement in these activities (Whitehead, 1990). She reads recipes, labels, timetables and instruction leaflets in the children's presence, she responds to their request to tell them 'What does this say?', and she encourages others to read those scripts and languages she cannot read herself (thereby emphasizing that Britain is a multilingual society and that others have skills which she does not). Similarly she demonstrates the ways in which she needs to write. The children when seeing her writing observations, reminder messages to herself, notices and labels, will inevitably ask 'What are you writing?' or 'What does that say?' or 'That letter's in my name.' These questions and comments provide the teacher with many opportunities for emphasizing the nature and uses of literacy skills.

Sometimes she will involve the children directly in her reading and writing activity. In one school some of the parents had been forgetting to close the high latch on the nursery gate. This meant that a child would be able to open the gate and get out into the street. The teacher decided to involve some of the children in addressing this problem. At the beginning of the morning session she sat down and talked with a small group of children in the graphics area. She explained about the gate and asked the children how they could remind the parents to close the top latch. Chantelle (aged 4 years) said 'Make a notice'. The process of deciding what the notice should say, how big it should be, making it, and deciding how and where to display it, and how to make it weather proof took up a large part of the morning. The children involved learnt not only about the uses of the written word, but also about mathematics (deciding on the notice's size and position) and about design features (how to weather-proof it). The teacher could have made the poster much more quickly alone, but she recognized the potential for learning during this activity. The poster was also more effective as a result of the children's direct involvement, because they were very eager to tell parents about it, and therefore reinforced the important message. Over the next few days, notices produced by individual children appeared all over the class, as children imitated what they had helped the teacher to do.

There are also many opportunities for teachers to demonstrate how they use mathematics in their daily life. Counting to see if they have enough money to buy the cooking ingredients, counting and dividing to see how many fish fingers each child can have at lunch time, using a calculator, measuring a space to see if a new piece of equipment will fit, weighing the bag of flour to see if there is enough for a recipe, cutting the fruit into pieces so there is enough for everyone and so on. These are real life experiences concerned with seeing mathematics as a tool, which children are also involved in at home, and are considerably more meaningful than the unrelated mathematics activities sometimes offered in school (Metz, 1987). Children are much more likely to demonstrate their mathematical ability when sharing out the cakes baked in a cookery session, than they would be during a formal bead counting activity. They are also more likely to want to try things which they have seen adults doing.

Many nursery teachers feel that, because they are women they were not encouraged to develop their scientific and technological understanding (Thomas, 1988), and have not developed the disposition to pursue these subjects. Some of them are, therefore, more nervous about acting as a role model in relation to these areas of the curriculum. Conscious of the need to give all children a broad experience, and of the fact that they are role models for the girls they teach, many teachers have taken steps to develop their confidence and expertise. Evening classes, in-service training, and learning alongside the children are all ways in which they have re-educated themselves. They have seen that it is not necessary for them to know all the answers. Their role is primarily to give children experience, and some understanding of scientific and technological processes. Above all they need to encourage children to make their own discoveries (Richards, 1987).

Every day in the nursery class opportunities for exploration and discovery of this kind are available. Through their own awareness, interest and willingness to investigate, teachers encourage children to ask questions such as 'Why has this container gone rusty?', and 'How could we stop the boat sinking?' and to explore problems such as 'Why does the bridge keep collapsing?' and 'How do you think you could make the boat move?' Children will gain inspiration from seeing their teachers ask questions and attempt to solve problems, as well as from adult demonstrations of skills. Many teachers mend and make equipment with the children, involving them fully in the process. Children's woodwork skills develop noticeably after they have worked with their teacher or another adult to make an item of equipment. The teacher does not need to be an expert. Through the use of reference books and plans, children can see again how literacy skills are applied, and any mistakes or problems can be worked on collaboratively. It may even be necessary to ask advice from someone with more experience.

Many adults make the mistake of thinking they need to know and be able to do everything. If they act as if this is the case, the children do not have the benefit of seeing an adult learner at work, and are given the impression that there comes a point in life when you stop learning. This is clearly not the case, and learning alongside adults is an important experience for young children. They are being offered some skills and some knowledge but, more importantly, they are being shown how to learn.

Many nursery staff and parents have creative talents which they share with the children. Seeing a talented artist or musician at work is undoubtedly inspiring for children. The children, whose teacher regularly played the piano to them, learnt a great deal about the use of this instrument. They could be observed imitating her use of the foot pedals, her hand and body movements, the way she played softly and loudly, and the way she turned the pages of the music she was using.

Similarly, seeing an adult paint, draw or use clay can also develop children's awareness of the possibilities for using these media. However, this should not be confused with adults drawing outlines for children to fill in, or pictures for children to copy. The talented artist who illustrates a poster for the school jumble sale in the children's presence is offering children the chance to see a more experienced person use their skill. On the other hand, the adult who draws or make pots for children to copy is undermining the children's skill, imposing ideas on them and limiting their imagination. From the first adult the children may take away those aspects of the experience which have personally inspired them – they are free to respond in their own way. The second adult expects all children to respond in the same way, and shows no respect for individual creativity. The first adult offers a stimulating role model, the second a stultifying template.

Adults also act as powerful role models when they sing, dance, tell (as opoposed to read) stories, use puppets and take on dramatic roles. In inspiring children to engage in these activities they are also encouraging their all-round development.

Adults have not always been seen as positive role models out of doors. As we saw in Chapter 3, some nursery teachers undervalue outdoor play and physical activity, and this negative attitude can result in nursery staff adopting a passive supervisory role out of doors. In developing equal opportunities policies some teams have recognized the need to get more involved in physical activity (Lally, 1986), both to prevent boys from dominating certain equipment and to encourage girls to develop the physical skills they need. This involvement includes joining in with throwing, climbing, hopping, etc., and making use of physical skills during gardening, building a low wall, and when retrieving a ball from the nursery roof. Seeing women engaged in vigorous, sometimes dirty, physical activity challenges the stereotyped views which even very young children hold.

Boys and girls of nursery age need to see both men and women involving themselves in the full range of activities. The minority of classes where both male and female staff are involved, work hard to make sure that all staff take equal responsibility for all tasks. In all classes, the teacher needs to ensure that parents are made aware of her objectives, and will want to encourage them to share their skills with the children. She will particularly want to encourage those parents who have developed interests and skills not usually associated with their gender to become involved – the father who works as a cook could be asked to lead some cooking sessions, the female plumber could be asked to talk with the children about her work and show them how she uses some of her tools and so on.

Teachers also believe it is important for adults involved with the nursery class to enable each other to tackle tasks they have not tried before. They therefore encourage those with skills to involve other adults as well as children. The example of the rabbit run which was referred to earlier was an example of this kind of collaboration. The nursery teacher in this case was the skilled carpenter, but through using a detailed plan containing instructions, and by offering verbal support she involved nursery nurses, parents and children in the project which took several days to complete.

This kind of apprenticeship model, where skills are demonstrated and shared, offers adults and children the chance to develop confidence as well as expertise. Enabling parents to work alongside their children in this way helps them to understand the teacher's approach and encourages them sometimes to take on the role of enabler in relation to staff. Many teachers and nursery nurses having access to computers for the first time have been grateful for the support of parents who work with computers and were able to offer advice. Parents also regularly take a lead in helping children and staff understand more about their religion, e.g. in one class Rheena (aged 4) was delighted to help her mother show a group of children, parents and staff how to make a rangoli pattern on the floor during Diwali.

Seeing their parents and the nursery staff working together in this way contributes to the children's self-esteem and security but, of course, teachers must ensure that all parents have the chance of involvement.

Some parents may not be able to spend time in school, but may be willing to arrange for a small group of children to visit them at work, or may be able to contribute items from work which are useful in school, such as old forms, X-ray plates and card. Those who speak languages other than English may be involved in supporting children who speak the same language in school and perhaps teaching the staff a few words. One teacher asked parents who spoke languages other than English if they would sing a song they had learnt in childhood onto a tape. The final collection included songs from France, Bangladesh, Vietnam, Jamaica, Iran, Italy and Pakistan. The parents involved, although shy at first, were encouraged by the teacher's enthusiasm and the interpreters' explanations, and thoroughly enjoyed trying to remember the words to songs from their past. The tape became a valuable and unique school resource.

It is the teacher's job to find ways for all parents to be involved positively in their child's school experience. This requires her to take a broad view of involvement which goes way beyond expecting parents to stay in the classroom. Her aim will always be to interest each parent in some aspect of school life which he or she is able to cope with, and build on that. The skilled teacher does not say things like 'the parents are not interested'. She knows that all parents are interested in their child in their own way, and that many of them wish to be more involved in their child's education (Smith, 1980; Tizard, Mortimore and Burchell, 1981). It is her responsibility to enable parents to take a role in their child's school experience.

Initiating Activities and Experiences

In the previous chapter the ways in which teachers plan specific activities or experiences for the children was described, and the difference between what the teacher plans and offers, and what is received by the children was highlighted. The following example demonstrates how a planned activity is adapted and developed to take account of the responses of individual children.

Natalie (3 years 7 months) and Terri (3 years 11 months) were close friends at school and nearly always played together. Both were receiving speech therapy for articulation difficulties, and the nursery staff had worked closely with both the children's therapists with a view to supporting the children's language development. The teacher had noticed that they were currently interested in water play, and her planned involvement for one morning was to be focused on the water tray. She intended to pursue their interest in transferring water from one container to another through the addition of equipment – sieves with different size holes, funnels, water wheels, guttering, tubing, spoons, different types of cloth, etc. – through posing challenges such as 'Can you find a way of getting the water from that container into that one without pouring it in?', and through a discussion of their discoveries. This could, of course, involve other children as well as Terri and Natalie.

However, on the morning of the activity snow had fallen (the first for over a year), and the teacher knew that this would be the major interest of the day. She also knew that, as the snow was not likely to settle for long, it was important to use this rare opportunity for learning from first-hand experience. This is the reality of 'following children's interests' – there is little point in following adult plans when the children's interest is elsewhere. If we truly believe that enthusiasm and motivation are important factors in learning we must not waste the opportunities which arise.

The teacher, therefore, met with the team before school started and together they planned and set up ways of exploring snow. Clean shovels and pattern making objects were placed in the snow covered garden, books (both fiction and reference) and relevant posters were prominently displayed, the tape and book of *The Snowman* (Briggs, 1978) were available to listen to on headphones and during a movement session. The nursery nurse planned to focus on feeding the birds and offered to make bird cake during the afternoon session to encourage the children to think about the effects of winter weather on other living creatures. The written plans were revised to take account of these changes.

The nursery teacher decided to postpone her planned activity. She knew that some children would come to school in shoes or clothing which would make it difficult for them to take part in outdoor exploration. In order to give these children the chance to find out about snow she decided to fill the water tray with snow instead of water. Before the children arrived she jotted down some of the discoveries which might be encouraged:

- The appearance of snow – the colour and shape of snowflakes (seen through a magnifying glass). What other substances does it look like?
- What does it feel like and what happens when we hold it in our hand? The concept of melting – in which conditions does snow melt quickly/slowly? Why has the snow in the water tray melted while the snow in the garden has not?
- What can you do with it? What effect do different tools (spades, rakes) have on it? Can it be used in a water wheel? Will it go through a funnel, etc.? Can we build with it?

The usual selection of water play equipment was available plus magnifying glasses and some transparent containers for use in melting experiments. However, the teacher intended to encourage sensory exploration before the use of equipment.

At the beginning of the morning session the teacher filled the tray with snow with the help of some of the children who had arrived early. She positioned herself near it. As expected, the majority of children wanted to play out of doors and most had arrived with wellington boots and suitable warm clothing to make this possible. However, Natalie and Terri, following the pattern of the last few days, headed immediately for the water tray. The unusual sight which greeted them stopped them in their tracks and Natalie exclaimed: 'Look Terri, there's snow!' The teacher responded, 'Yes, come and find out what it feels like.' Natalie walked on past the tray to the shelves of equipment and called back over her shoulder to the teacher 'It's cold,' and proceeded to collect a jug. She went to the classroom sink and filled it with water. Terri copied her. They returned to the water tray and started to pour the water over the snow. As they did so, they noticed that, as the water landed on the surface of the snow, holes appeared. Almost simultaneously they shouted, 'Look, I've made a hole.'

This development was one which had not been anticipated by the teacher – it did not feature in her plans! There are many occasions like this where teachers of young children have a choice to make. They can either attempt to focus the children on their plans (and run the risk of losing the children's interest), or they can respond to the children's enthusiasm. The latter choice requires quick and flexible thinking on the part of the teacher.

In this particular case, she had to respond enthusiastically to the children's discovery, even though she was aware that the snow would soon be water. After sharing their initial excitement, she had to help them sustain their interest and extend their understanding of what was happening by quickly thinking up and offering a set of challenges such as:

- I wonder what would happen if we pour the water very slowly or drip it through a pipette or syringe?
- How else could we make holes in the snow?
- What would happen if we used hot water?

By valuing the children's discovery and helping them to explore it further through the investigations she suggested, she sustained their interest and created a positive – enjoyable but demanding – environment for learning. She took some photographs of their experience both to remind them and to share with other children.

What the children actually learnt is more difficult to determine but the teacher is given clues by their comments. They may not yet understand why, but they undoubtedly knew that hot water had a different effect on the snow than cold water. They learnt the word for steam and their awareness had also been heightened. The teacher noted that later that morning Terri and Natalie could be seen showing the nursery nurse how drips of melting snow from the roof of the playhouse were making holes in the snow on the grass below. Above all, they had been encouraged through this experience to express their discoveries in complex spoken language – which was, after all, one of the teacher's original intentions and they had been encouraged to set up investigations.

Surely this is how we all learn. From our first-hand experiences and explorations we gradually gain a clearer picture of the world, and are able to make connections between one experience and another. Communicating our experiences to others takes our learning a stage further as we struggle to describe what happened to someone else who may not have been involved. The skill of the teacher lies in offering inspiring experiences, sustaining interest, and helping children to find some possible explanations for their own discoveries.

Merely offering experiences and activities is relatively simple. What distinguishes the skilled nursery teacher from other under-5s' practitioners is her ability to take her lead from the children, to see ways of maximizing the interest they are showing and to enable them to relate one experience to another. There is also skill involved in knowing when to stop – recognizing the point at which the question you have posed is outside the interest or understanding of the child.

At the end of each observation or interaction, the teacher records the knowledge and skills each child demonstrated and also what she has learnt about each child's dispositions and feelings. It is just as important to record that Natalie and Terri had the confidence to pursue their own intentions and responded enthusiastically to the teacher's challenges, as it is to record that they were able to describe some of the properties of snow, and could skilfully pour water quickly and slowly. It was also important to record how they were able to refer back to their discoveries later that morning, and how they were able to remember enough to dictate captions for the teacher to write next to the photographs when they were developed a week later.

Demonstrating Skills and Imparting Knowledge

Of course, there are occasions when the teacher will want to teach more directly. Children need certain skills and knowledge and there are times when it is appropriate to show them how to do something or tell them the information they need. Once again it is essential that the teacher carefully selects the moment for intervention of this kind. The learner is most likely to achieve a skill or take in new knowledge within a context which has motivated him to learn and with an adult who is encouraging and supportive (EYCG, 1989).

Sometimes a child will ask directly for help. Young children learning to use scissors will often ask an adult to hold the paper or fabric they wish to cut, knowing that they can achieve this task with help. They may also ask 'What is this?' or 'What's that called?' in relation to new equipment, giving the teacher a clue that they are ready for this knowledge. Children are avid namers of things and particularly enjoy learning unusual words – of all the new musical instruments in one class, the guiro and the cabasa were the names most quickly learnt.

Teachers will also use opportunities when children make a mistake to help them develop new knowledge and skills. The child who rushes up to the teacher holding a beetle and says 'Look, I've found a spider,' will be helped to understand the similarities and differences between a beetle and a spider, perhaps with the help of a book. The teacher who replies 'It's not a spider, it's a beetle', would not take the child's knowledge further because she would not have helped the child to understand why it was not a spider. She may also have inhibited the child from sharing ideas with her in the future. By acknowledging the similarities the child has seen and then helping him to identify some of the differences, the teacher encourages the child's own ideas and shows him ways of investigating them.

Young children often have ideas which they do not have the skills or knowledge to execute. They often become frustrated as their attempts end in failure. They may ask adults for help, or may accept the help of an adult who has observed their difficulty. In both cases, the teacher has the opportunity to teach new skills and knowledge. Lynne (3 years 7 months) wanted to stick a cardboard tube onto a box. She had been applying the glue to the sides of the tube rather than to the part she actually wanted to stick. She called to her teacher 'Glue won't stick.' The teacher was able to explain to her that the glue had to be applied to the surface you want to stick. With this information Lynne was able to continue her project.

Anita (4 years 8 months) had spent most of the morning building herself a house from milk crates. She wanted to make a roof and had selected a blanket to place over the top. However the house was too wide and the blanket kept sagging into the house. Each time it sagged she put it back on again. After three attempts she was visibly upset. The teacher noticed this and approached her as she started to put the blanket back for the fourth time. She asked, 'Have you got a problem?' Anita replied tearfully: 'The blanket keeps falling down.' The teacher suggested she weighted the blanket down at the edges. This was enough support to enable Anita to solve her problem. She got some solid wooden bricks and was able to continue her game successfully.

Through watching children engaged in activities they have chosen themselves, teachers can select the most receptive times for this kind of help. The moment to help a child form letters correctly is when she is attempting to write her name, just as tidying up time is the moment to show a child how to use the brush and dustpan effectively. These moments can also be planned for. Teachers can suggest that a child writes his name on his painting or drawing in order to be able to help with letter formation, or she can ask a small group of children to help her put away the bricks in order to check which shapes they know, and to introduce new names. It is these meaningful, pleasurable contexts for learning new skills and knowledge which the teacher exploits to the full.

The Teacher as Playmate

So far the focus has been on the ways in which teachers put their plans into action to enable learning to take place. This is only part of the nursery curriculum as we have seen, with many planned activities having to be revised. If teachers are to respond to individual needs they also need to make time for spontaneous involvement in children's play. Teacher's with the personal qualities described earlier in this chapter will find that they are often asked by children to join in – through requests to come and have 'dinner' in the home corner, or to come shopping on the 'bus', or to be the patient in the 'hospital' or to have a story 'read' to them. Teachers know that these are some of the most valuable opportunities they have to gain more insight into children's thoughts and feelings and, consequently, join in readily.

Sometimes the teacher is not invited by the children, and has to find her own way of being involved. If she wishes to avoid rejection, she needs to listen and observe in order to find a natural role for herself. The teacher who walks into a situation where children are doing each other's hair and asks 'What are you doing?' is less likely to be enthusiastically received, than the teacher who asks 'Can I make an appointment to have my hair washed and cut please?' This is because the first teacher is remaining aloof from the situation, while the second shows value for the activity and involves herself directly in it. The first is being the 'teacher' while the second is offering herself as a playmate.

Teachers use their incidental observations to give them clues about where they need to involve themselves spontaneously, and what the purpose of this involvement should be. They also draw on their knowledge of individual children to help them decide how they should approach a particular situation. The following examples are provided to give some insight into different approaches to involvement in play.

Encouraging Imitation

The teacher will often engage in parallel play with a child to offer him or her a role model. The child whose language development is delayed may need help in order to put actions into words. Without this skill he or she will find it difficult to relate to others.

Fergus (3 years 4 months) was playing alone in the home corner. The teacher, who was concerned about his speech which even his parents found difficult to understand, observed him put a doll to bed. She went into the home corner with a doll and said:

'My baby's tired. I'm going to put her to bed.'
Fergus: 'Baby bed.'
Teacher: 'There. My baby's in bed like yours.'
She tucked in the blankets. Fergus copied.
Teacher: 'My baby's asleep now. Is yours?'
Fergus: 'Baby see.' (Asleep.)
Teacher: 'Shh. We'd better be quiet now.'
Fergus: 'Ssss' putting his finger on his lips.

This short, pleasurable interlude gave Fergus the opportunity to play with someone else. Although he was unable to take a lead he was able to respond to the teacher in a meaningful way. He was being offered some words to describe his actions in a relaxed, meaningful context. The next day he approached the teacher again holding a doll and said 'Ssss. Baby see.'

Other times when the teacher joins in play with a view to encouraging imitation are usually to demonstrate more appropriate use of equipment. Joanne (3 years 6 months) was using a saw but had not placed her piece of wood in the clamp on the workbench. Her teacher went over to the bench and showed her how to place the wood in the clamp explaining how it kept the wood still. She used this opportunity to saw a shelf which had been waiting to be cut down to size, so that she could work alongside Joanne and help her consolidate her new skill.

Broadening Knowledge

Teachers regularly join in activities with the intention of broadening the children's knowledge through play rather than by direct instruction.

A 'dentist's surgery' had been set up following the visit of the school dentist, but it was clear that the children seemed to think that you went to the dentist only to have teeth out. The teacher made an appointment to see the 'dentist' for a check up, asking the child at 'reception' to write down the details for her. When receiving her treatment, she was able to extend the children's limited knowledge by suggesting things to them such as 'I'm a bit worried about my filling. Can you look with your mirror to see if it's come loose?' (When the child said it had to come out she said 'No, I don't want it taken out yet, I'd like you to put another filling in it please'); 'Has your nurse written down that my teeth are alright?'; and 'Have you got a glass of water I can rinse my mouth out with please?'

Similarly, by playing the part of a customer in a shop or at the post office, a passenger on a bus or train, or a client at the hairdresser's, the teacher can broaden the children's knowledge of what is involved in a variety roles. For example, by going into the 'post office' and asking for a form for a passport, the teacher helps children to understand that the post office does not just involve letters and stamps.

Posing Problems and Extending Thinking

Often when she is involved in children's play the teacher is able to see or experience problems which they have not anticipated. By drawing their attention to these problems she is able to extend their thinking, and what was a lighthearted episode can sometimes become a rigorous intellectual activity.

One teacher had been invited on a 'journey' with a group of three children who were being led by Emily and Elisabetta (both 4 years of age). Both children had recently returned from holidays abroad and both had vivid imaginations. The 'journey' involved making full use of the outdoor play equipment to travel around the world. The playhouse became the aeroplane, some milk crates a train and the playbox a bus. After using each of these modes of transport and visiting all the countries the children could name, the travellers finally came to what Emily described as 'A very dangerous river. It's got crocodiles and snakes in it so you'd better be very careful.' She instructed the group to get across the river by straddling a plank which made a bridge between two metal supports. The children went first followed by the teacher, who quickly discovered that she could not sit straddling the plank without her feet touching the ground (going in the water). She called out 'Help! My legs are too long. I can't keep them out of the water.' This captured the children's imagination and they quickly came to her aid. They all returned to the 'shore' to tackle the problem. After much discussion they decided the teacher would have to crawl across the plank on her tummy! Many of the problems which arise when adults join in play are concerned with size, and solving them provides valuable mathematical experience as well as opportunites to work co-operatively. It is worth noting that many companies spend vast amounts of money sending their staff on 'team-building' courses which involve very similar problem solving activities.

Teachers also intervene to help children think in more depth about the way they represent things in play. Following a visit by a police horse and rider Adrian (4 years 6 months) and David (4 years 8 months) were reliving the experience. Adrian was moving around the playground on his hands and knees, and David was walking beside him pretending to beat him with a the inner tube from a kitchen roll (they had not observed the police officer doing this). David said to his teacher: 'Look at my horse.' Knowing that these children benefited from being encouraged to think in more depth she replied 'Is he like the police horse?' David looked at Adrian for a moment, giggled, and said: 'No, he hasn't got a tail.' The teacher asked if there were any other differences and Adrian said 'No tongue.' (The tongue had been an important feature of the police horse because it was large and seemed to produce a lot of dribble as it ate an apple.) Without any further prompting, the children rushed inside and when they came out later Adrian had a paper tail, a card tongue (which they had stuck to his tongue with Sellotape!) and two, pointed card ears. The nursery nurse reported that they had spent a considerable length of time selecting materials, cutting them to shape and size and deciding how to attach them.

Intervention of this kind must be informed by the teacher's knowledge of individual children, since it is just as easy for adults to bring play to an end as it is to move it forward.

Challenging Stereotyped Ideas

It is clearly important that teachers encourage children to develop a broad view of society. In order to achieve this they need to listen to the children and intervene if stereotyped ideas are being put forward.

Tamsin (aged 3½) announced loudly to Luke and Clare 'Girls can't be the doctor.' The teacher asked her why not and, when she replied 'They can't', reminded her that the school doctor (whom she saw the previous week) was a woman. She also made a point of reading a book involving a female doctor at story time.

Teachers have to monitor carefully the kinds of play they involve them-selves in to be sure that they are not reinforcing gender stereotypes. For example, too much involvement in domestic play at the expense of con-struction and vigorous outdoor play gives powerful messages to all children about female roles. Similar stereotyping occurs if male staff are seen to be the ones who are always involved in rough and tumble play.

Involvement in play can, incidentally, alert teachers to other prejudices children may hold, and enables them to tackle this with the children con-cerned. Negative attitudes towards black dolls, images in posters, or to-wards other children in the class, will often be expressed innocently at this stage and teachers are given many opportunities to encourage children to reconsider.

Andrew (3 years 6 months) was playing with a small group and the teacher at the dough table. A display nearby showed photographs of a cooking session which had been led by a Vietnamese parent. Looking at the pictures Andrew announced 'I don't like that food. It's yukky.' His teacher tackled this by checking whether he had tried the food in the picture and when he said no, told him that she had, and that it had been delicious. She told him that he would only know if he liked it if he had tried it. She also pointed out to him that other children could be seen enjoying the food in the picture. It was therefore not true to say the food was 'yukky' just because he thought he did not like it. She told him about some food she disliked, but made the point that just because she disliked it did not mean she called it 'yukky'. Other children were present during this discussion and the teacher was interested to overhear one of them telling another child at lunchtime not to call something 'yukky' just 'cos you don't like it'.

These are the kinds of discussions referred to in Chapter 2 and are essential if we are serious about confronting racism and sexism.

Moving on Repetitive Play

Sometimes teachers will want to involve themselves because they have observed that some children's play has become repetitive and is limiting their ability to try other activities. This can be because a child lacks confidence and has found security in one activity.

Amy (3 years 4 months) had attended nursery for half a term and rarely ventured out of the art and craft workshop. She enjoyed using the range of painting, collage and junk materials to construct and create, but the nursery team were beginning to feel she was using the enclosed area as a shelter from the rest of the nursery class. The teacher made a point of working alongside her and was able to draw her out of the area briefly to find other materials for her creation. Gradually with support over a period of weeks, Amy gained enough confidence to venture out alone.

In other cases, groups of children establish a pattern of behaviour in school which they cannot break. Often these group games are inspired by television programmes and more often than not involve boys chasing each other and/or 'shooting' each other. This type of play is not the kind of educational play which teachers wish to encourage, and yet it often seems to motivate the children more than anything else. Many teachers observe this play to try to discover what it is that the children enjoy – is it the chasing, the shooting, the shouting or . . .? If they understand what is motivating the children they are better placed to extend the activity, or offer an equally exciting alternative. Setting up a space station in one class transformed what had been largely aggressive space play into a more varied, technological learning experience. As the children's interest developed so the aggressive incidents decreased.

The aim here has been to show how teachers work from the children's current interests to move them forwards. Abruptly stopping them from doing the things they want to do is usually counterproductive as anyone who has ever told children they are not to make guns in the nursery will know! It merely results in them keeping their concerns hidden from adults. A more effective way is to show interest in what they are doing and offer them exciting, related alternatives.

Understanding Children

All of the above examples have emphasized the way in which a teacher can gain insight into a child's interests and ideas through her involvement in their play. Although the teacher will sometimes intervene with the intention of influencing the play, there are also times when she will allow the children to take the lead and will merely observe, listen and join in in the ways they ask her to. Those uninhibited teachers, who can really get into a role in play, are the ones the children relax with and are therefore the ones who gain the greatest insights.

Responsive teaching depends on teachers understanding their pupils. It requires teachers to value the children's concerns, and to acknowledge the potential for learning within activities the children have chosen themselves. Teachers who work in the sensitive ways described above demonstrate that they value the children's ideas. They are usually able to offer suggestions and ask questions in ways which children want to respond to. When children do not respond they know they have got their approach wrong and need to learn from their mistake.

The idea that children as young as 3 and 4 have anything to teach adults is difficult for some people to grasp, and yet we only have to listen to a 3-year-old for a short while to realize that as adults our view of the world has often become very narrow, and has been hardened by experience. If we are to support rather than limit children's developing understanding, we need to allow them to help us recapture some of the wonder and innocence we have lost. Teaching is not about imposing our views, concerns or values on others. It is about enabling children to carry out their own investigations and make up their own minds. They have already begun to do this before they come to school. The nursery teacher makes it possible for them to continue in the school situation.

Some Points for Discussion

Acting as a Role Model

Ask yourself honestly:

- What kind of person am I? For example, am I gregarious or shy, confident or timid, open or afraid of discussing feelings, eager to try new things and meet new people or nervous about new experiences, positive or negative, and so on?
- Do I enjoy playing with young children or do I feel uncomfortable in this

role? It is important to understand ourselves if we are to understand our relationships with others, and to evaluate whether we are suited to a particular role.

- What kind of an example am I and other members of the team setting the children in our class? For example, are we encouraging them by our example to be kind, calm, excitable, enthusiastic, noisy, adventurous, etc.?
- Are they learning to have a go, to believe that girls cannot do some things, to behave inappropriately to gain attention, to listen or ignore?
- What kind of role models do you want to be?
- How can you make sure you all achieve this?

Involvement in Learning Experiences

How do you enable learning to take place in your class? Make a list of some of the things you do, say, and provide to stimulate interest, and to support and extend learning. Think about your recent involvement with the children and remember actual incidents – identify the different kinds of support you offered. What was successful/unsuccessful? Why? How do you make sure that all children are supported?

What is the balance of time you spend involved with activities you have initiated, compared with the time you spend observing and joining in with child-initiated activity?

From your own observations, can you identify features of the kinds of learning contexts and adult interactions which most effectively stimulate and sustain the children's interest? What conclusions can you draw from this about:

- How children learn?
- The role of the adult in children's learning?

How could you share this understanding with colleagues, governors and parents?

6

THE NURSERY TEACHER AS A COMMITTED, SELF-CRITICAL ENTHUSIAST

The aim of this book has been to describe the complexity involved in the education of young children, and to highlight the expertise of the nursery teacher. One major question remains however. If she is so highly skilled, why has it been so difficult for the teacher to act as an advocate for her profession? Some possible answers to this question have already been suggested in earlier chapters, most notably the general lack of respect given to those who are involved with young children. However, part of the answer rests with the teacher herself.

When listening to groups of teachers in discussion, it becomes apparent that the most effective ones seem to be the most critical of themselves and of their work. These teachers are aware of the demands they are facing, and are conscious that they will never be able to do the job as well as they would like. They know, for example, that responsiveness to individuals is only as possible as staffing ratios allow. In spite of this frustration they generally do not become disillusioned – on the contrary, they constantly strive to improve their practice. This seems to be largely because of their commitment to offering the young children in their classes the best possible education.

The knowledge that there is always room for improvement tends to make teachers too modest about their achievements. If they can be persuaded to talk about their strengths they tend to counter these immediately with a list of weaknesses! In this chapter we take a look at some of the issues which teachers are grappling with, with a view to explaining this modesty and reluctance to talk about achievements.

Teaching as Personal Development

The approach to the education of young children described in earlier chapters requires the teacher to evaluate and adapt her practice in response to her own observations and to the wealth of research evidence available to her. This includes early learning research, the implications of which have been referred to earlier. However, a responsive approach to children also requires teachers to develop their knowledge and understanding of the social context within which they are educating, in particular, how developments in society influence the lives of the families they work with.

In placing the needs of children at the centre of the curriculum, teachers must regularly confront their own assumptions and prejudices. Teaching is still a predominantly white, middle class profession. It is not unusual for a young teacher from a sheltered middle class background to find herself working in an inner-city school with children from social and cultural backgrounds outside her personal experience. This is because the provision of nursery schools and classes 'is higher in deprived areas and in urban areas, and lower in more affluent areas and in rural areas' (ESAC, 1989). It is also because, due to the shortage of nursery education places, priority is often given (particularly in nursery schools) to socially disadvantaged children and those 'living in poor neighbourhoods' (Osborn and Milbank, 1987, p. 92).

Initial training courses must, therefore, help student teachers to begin the often painful self-evaluation process. Students need to be helped to see that they have formed a set of attitudes and values based on their own life experience, and that these are not necessarily shared by others. They also need to recognize that attitudes and values are not fixed – teachers must be prepared to question themselves in the light of new experiences and alternative points of view. Attitudes and values associated with childrearing, discipline, cleanliness, the roles of men and women, living in a multicultural society, etc., are acquired consciously and unconsciously from birth. They are expressed in our work – 'not explicitly for the most part, but implicitly, in the thousands of judgements and decisions that we make in the course of a single day' (Drummond, Lally and Pugh, 1989).

Unless we make ourselves aware of our own beliefs and the reasons we acquired them, we run the risk of communicating 'values and attitudes which may not only be unfamiliar to many children but may also seem to reject their own experiences' (Hazareesingh, Simms and Anderson, 1989,

p. 24). Whether we question ourselves or are challenged by others, the process of understanding the nature and origins of our own attitudes can be a painful one – it is after all disturbing to realize that some of the attitudes we hold are racist or sexist. Discussing attitudes and values with others, who do not share our beliefs, is also difficult and can feel threatening, and yet it is often through discussion with someone who holds a conflicting point of view, that we are able to clarify our thinking and reach new insights.

Nursery teachers, in the course of their work, will be confronted with a range of different views held by their colleagues, by parents and by members of the school community. Their own attitudes will equally be laid open to question. The broader their own view of possible viewpoints the more sensitive they will be to others. A collaborative approach to early education requires teachers to respond in full to the questions of others. It is not appropriate for them to say 'this is how we do things in this nursery' (or words to that effect) without giving any reasons. The more successfully teachers involve parents and community members in the life of the nursery class, the more questions will be asked – in the same way that the more teachers encourage children to negotiate with others, the more they will negotiate with adults. It is essential that teachers are able to respond to these approaches confidently and do not become defensive because they feel their position is threatened.

Tutors on initial and in-service courses have a responsibility to help teachers to face up to the 'why' questions which will be asked of them. They need to see that these questions represent a genuine and legitimate interest – a very real desire to know more – and that the content of the inquiries will change over time to take into account developments in society. For example, nursery teachers now find themselves being asked about the National Curriculum as parents seek to ensure their children are given the best possible start.

Most of all, teachers need to know that they must review and sometimes change their attitudes – not so that they blindly take on board every other attitude they are exposed to, but in a thoughtful way to show respect for the concerns of others even when attitudes cannot be shared. The teacher who listens to, and shows some understanding for, the parent who is concerned that her 3-year-old son likes dressing up in skirts, is more likely to be able to allay that parent's fears, than the teacher who dismisses the concern and leaves no room for discussion.

As we saw in Chapter 3, an ability to respect others depends on self-awareness. This is as true for the teacher as it is for a child. The more they confront themselves, the less likely teachers are to be afraid of the questions of others. If they allow themselves to learn from the children and parents they come into contact with in the ways described in Chapter 5, they will have many opportunities to reflect on their own assumptions, and will be offered many different, and often equally valid, ways of looking at the world.

Teaching in a Developing Society

Teachers who have been involved in nursery education for the last ten years or more, talk enthusiastically about the ways in which they have developed as people, and the ways in which their practice has changed. It is the dynamic nature of nursery teaching, and the relationships teachers develop with families, which help teachers to maintain their commitment to this work in spite of the low status and lack of real career prospects. In fact, some teachers are committed to nursery teaching precisely because it offers the opportunity for personal development via community involvement. On being told she might have to transfer to the infant class of her school because of teacher shortages, one teacher explained how she would be devastated to lose contact with the families she had built up such warm relationships with. She recognized that this kind of contact is not generally possible with the less favourable adult/child ratios in the infant school.

In recent years educational, political and sociological factors have influenced the way in which the nursery teacher approaches her work. Changes in practice related to curriculum development have already been described in earlier chapters, but many teachers also believe that they have developed personally through becoming more aware of issues such as discrimination, changing family composition and childrearing practices and so on. These issues are examined below.

Discrimination in British Society

Through their involvement with families from a variety of social and cultural backgrounds, teachers have had to face up to the inequalities based on class, culture, gender and disability which exist in British society. Daily, teachers are exposed to questions such as 'Why do black families suffer disproportionately from low incomes, poor housing, and unemployment?' (Commission for Racial Equality, 1977) and why is it nearly always the women whose job prospects suffer because of child-care responsibilities? Seeing for themselves how families cope with situations, which they themselves would find impossible, is a powerful learning experience for teachers – it certainly forces them to re-think many of their own expectations.

How can you expect a child to be in bed early when he is living with his parents and sister in one small room in bed and breakfast accommodation? Or, how can you expect a lone mother to arrive on time to collect her child every day when she is trying to hold down a low paid job within the few hours her child is able to attend nursery class? Many teachers have become vocal advocates of extended day provision because they are aware of the difficulties involved in finding jobs which fit in with the school day or, even worse, half day. Similarly, teachers have had to ask themselves whether they, through their actions, interactions or practice are adding to the discrimination experienced by some families. Many are currently concerned about the inequalities experienced by those families who speak a language other than English at home – how is it possible to make sure that these families gain equal access to information and have the same opportunities to share their feelings with nursery staff when the support of translators and interpreters for all the required languages is often impossible to come by?

Family Composition

The traditional idea of the family as two parents and two children with a network of grandparents, aunts, uncles and cousins living nearby for support, is rapidly becoming a myth. Many children currently live in one-parent families (usually with their mother), and many have been involved in family breakdown – Britain currently has one of the highest divorce rates in Europe – and in subsequently formed stepfamilies (Wicks, 1989). The numbers of children born outside marriage is increasing (Family Policy Studies Centre, 1990) although many of these children are registered and brought up by both parents. Families are likely to be more mobile (ESAC, 1989) and less likely (particulary in the south east of England) to live as part of an extended family with grandparents nearby to offer support.

Teachers must take account of these trends when working with children and must not make assumptions (such as the assumption that every child has a dad at home) or value judgements about family structure (for example, that a two parent family is more stable than a one parent family). Through contact with actual families they see for themselves that many different kinds of family structure work well.

Childrearing Practices

Traditional attitudes to childrearing have been challenged by changes in family composition, and by the traditions of the many ethnic groups living in Britain. Teachers, through discussion with parents, can make themselves aware of differences in childrearing practice, and about pressures on parents, and avoid judging some practices negatively. 'There is no single "best" way to bring up a child, and there are as many differences in childrearing practices among white and among black families as there are between them' (Commission for Racial Equality, 1990). Teachers need, in their initial training courses, to learn to respect and value these differences, and to understand the importance of gaining concrete information about each child's background and experiences (Hazareesingh, Simms and Anderson, 1989).

Attitudes to childrearing are influenced by the political priorities of the day. During the Second World War, when women were needed in the workforce, it was considered acceptable for children to be cared for in nurseries. After the war with the men returned and wanting their jobs back, the nurseries were closed and women encouraged to see their role back in the home (Riley, 1983). A similar but, perhaps, more ambivalent pattern is currently emerging. Women are needed in and being urged to join the workforce, and yet there is still the prevailing view that they are responsible for childcare and must make their own private arrangements with the help of employers and the voluntary sector. Teachers, who see for themselves the stress caused to many young families by this ambivalence, are less likely to make sweeping judgements about working women and more likely to campaign for the full and extended day provision families need.

The Role of Women in Society

In some ways the teacher is as much a victim of discrimination as many of the women she works with. Work with young children is still seen as women's work, even though the numbers of male nursery teachers and nursery nurses is increasing steadily. Indeed, parents often consider nursery teachers to be less able than teachers of older children – many teachers report that a move into the infant department is seen as promotion! There are currently two strands to the campaign to raise the status of women. First, the effort and skills involved in caring for children need to be recognized and valued. It should no longer be the norm for women to devalue themselves with phrases like 'I'm just a housewife' or 'I'm only a nursery teacher'. Second, women need to be helped to believe that they are capable of achieving outside the home, if that is what they want to do.

Clearly, the nursery teacher, because of her involvement with mothers of young children, has a role to play in both these areas. Her attitude to herself as a woman will determine how much she is able to support the women she comes into contact with. She needs to believe in herself, and value her own achievements in order to be confident enough to encourage others to value themselves and try new things. In response to this challenge and to parents' requests, teachers in some schools have organized adult education classes to be run during nursery hours to enable women to develop new skills. Alternatively, or alongside these classes, support groups for parents focusing on the parenting role have also been set up, to offer participants the chance to discuss with others (with and without professional involvement) the pleasures and problems involved in bringing up children. Clearly, space is an issue here, but a growing awareness of the needs of parents has prompted many nursery teachers to make a strong case for the extra space and resources required to respond to these needs. Spare classrooms, portacabins in playgrounds and even staff rooms are all being used to facilitate support of these kinds (Pugh and De'Ath, 1989).

Child Abuse

Child abuse is certainly not a new development in society, but the numbers of reported cases has definitely increased in recent years, and awareness of the problem has been heightened. The latest research (NSPCC, 1990, p. 14) indicates 'a 35 per cent increase in the number of children added to child protection registers, a 100 per cent increase in the number of children registered for emotional abuse', and 'a 66 per cent increase in registrations in the "grave concern" category'. It is not yet entirely clear whether these increases represent an actual increase in the number of children who have been abused, or whether they are the result of increased awareness and vigilance on the part of the general public and childcare professionals.

Children under the age of 4 are most vulnerable (Renvoize, 1974) and some start nursery class with their names already on the child protection register. Others rely on nursery staff to pick up the signs. In response to a growing awareness of the nature and extent of abuse (including sexual abuse), local authorities have organized training courses for those working with young children, to help them to identify signs of abuse and to inform them of the procedures they need to follow if abuse is suspected. Many of these courses bring professionals from different statutory and voluntary services together, and all local authorities have published guidelines for their staff to follow.

Acknowledging the fact that young children suffer physical, emotional and sexual abuse has been difficult for many nursery staff. Most of us would prefer to believe that such things could never happen. At the same time, teachers have been made to realize that they are often in a key position to offer support to a child. It is their responsibility to monitor behaviour, to notice any suspicious injuries and to listen carefully to what the children say. If there is any reason at all to suspect that a child may have been abused then this must be reported. Being aware that this action must be taken makes it virtually impossible knowingly to turn away from the issue.

Nevertheless, this is probably one of the most stressful responsibilities any teacher can hold. If she (and her team) fail to notice the signs, the child risks further abuse, and yet if she gets it wrong her relationship with a family is put at risk. Some teachers honestly admit to the anguish they go through when trying to decide whether or not to report something they have seen or heard. Some cases are clear cut – the child with the very obvious cigarette burns – while others are less so – the rather sad, pale and withdrawn child. Teachers know that if they report a suspicion, they will set in motion a chain of social work, and probably police inquiries, which will irrevocably change their relationship with a family. Those who have reported their suspicions have often felt deeply distressed even though they know they have acted properly.

Working with children and parents where abuse has been proved also causes anxiety. Continuing to support a parent abuser, when you really want to despise her is a dilemma all professionals involved in child protection work have to face. Child abuse brings us all in touch with very powerful emotions, and teachers have to cope with their own feelings as well as with helping other members of staff and sometimes other parents cope with theirs. It is also quite possible that a member of staff was abused herself, and is being reminded of what happened to her. Working with abused children who may talk about, or act out what has happened to them, often leaves staff feeling inadequate. Their training does not on the whole equip them to deal with these very difficult and often distressing situations.

Many teachers have very wisely obtained support through their contacts with other professionals involved in child protection and family support work, such as health visitors, school nurses and doctors, social workers and educational welfare officers – it is, after all, considerably easier to discuss suspicions with someone you know who also knows and cares about a family. These interagency links are a growing feature of nursery education. They have often developed as a result of the teacher's awareness of her role within the total support network for families – she knows that she needs to draw on the expertise of others if she is to be able to offer informed support to children and their families. As a teacher, her training is limited and there are times when she needs to refer a parent or child to another professional or agency (Dowling, 1988). She also needs the support of others to help her cope with her responsibilities and the feelings these generate.

All of these human issues have caused the teacher to reflect on her own attitudes and feelings and, as we have seen, this is sometimes a painful process. Less painful, but equally demanding, are the technological and political issues she has to address in her work.

Technological Advances

Young children are growing up in an increasingly technological society. A considerable amount of their leisure time is spent watching television or video programmes – some of the programmes not entirely appropriate for children under 5. Some children have access to a home computer. Nursery teachers, many of whom admit they lack confidence when faced with machinery, have had to recognize that they must build on the experience children are gaining at home (Dowling, 1988; Broom, 1990), since this generation of under-5s, more than any other, is seeing, and needs to continue to see, technology as an everyday part of their lives. It is not possible to predict what these youngsters will be using when they are adults, but we do know the advances are likely to continue, and that many machines we use now are likely to be obsolete.

The effects of television and video viewing on young children are apparent on any visit to a nursery class. Groups of children are often involved in playing out a scene from their favourite programme, and lunchtime discussions often focus on what was seen the night before, such as the discussion of an episode of *EastEnders* which involved one 4-year-old girl in announcing animatedly 'I'm not having a baby 'cos you gotta push, push!' There is little doubt that many programmes are not fully understood and can have a profound, even if temporary, effect on these young viewers. One of the major challenges facing teachers and parents involves finding ways of countering some of the negative effects of television viewing. Many teachers try to watch some of the programmes enjoyed by the children at home so that they can join in discussion and extend the children's understanding of the programmes.

Not all children have the benefit of viewing programmes with a sympathetic adult, and one of the reasons teachers give for using television in the nursery class is their concern to give children the chance to view critically with an adult. They believe that helping children to discuss and evaluate what they see will help them to select and reject programmes for themselves. They stress that the content of programmes viewed should be relevant to the children's current interests, and that only small groups of

children should be involved – whole class viewing is believed to be counterproductive because it discourages interaction and discussion. Other
teachers believe that children watch enough television at home and need
other experiences in nursery.

A similar polarization of views is associated with the use of computers by
nursery age children. Some teachers feel that computers rely too much on
abstract symbols, and have no place in nursery education where the emphasis is on real life experience. A growing view, however, is that computers are a part of children's real life experience, and that, as long as
teachers select software carefully in line with their principles, they can add
a new dimension to the children's learning – particularly in the area of
problem solving (Broom, 1990).

In order to respond to technological advances most teachers have had to
overcome their own anxieties and learn new skills. Some have attended
computer literacy courses, and a few have learnt to use video equipment, so
that they can show the children what is involved in film making. It is
perhaps in this area of the curriculum more than any other that teachers
have needed to learn alongside the children. This is by no means a disadvantage, since, as we saw earlier, children benefit greatly from working
alongside an adult who is demonstrating how to investigate problems, test
theories and seek support.

Nursery Education and Politics

As one experienced teacher commented to a group of probationers 'when
you become a nursery teacher you also become a campaigner – the two
roles go together'. The reality of working in the non-statutory sector, where
nothing (not even the continued existence of your class) can be taken for
granted, is the inevitable involvement (either conscious or unconscious) of
the nursery teacher in politics. More and more teachers have become
consciously involved during the last few years as the spotlight has fallen on
provision for the under-5s, and another call for an expansion of nursery
education (ESAC, 1989) seems to have been ignored.

This involvement takes the form of working through lobbying organizations, such as the National Campaign for Nursery Education (NCNE), or
through charitable organizations such as the British Association for Early
Childhood Education (BAECE), and includes local as well as national
activity. Essentially, teachers always have to be aware of local and national
developments which may affect their employment prospects, and the future of the children they teach. Developments such as a change of political
control at local or national level, or the need to cut local authority budgets,

or to redeploy teachers into the statutory sector to counter teacher shortages, or the decision to admit all 4-year-olds to reception classes, can all have serious implications for nursery education. Teachers have a responsibility to make themselves and others aware of these developments, and to put forward a strong case. Some parents are unaware of the vulnerability of nursery education, particularly if they have always lived in an area with good provision, and often need to be told that it is not their child's automatic right. When faced with the prospect of transferring their child to infant school, at what seems to them a very young age, they also need advice. They need to know that they are not legally obliged to send their child to school until the beginning of the term after his or her fifth birthday. Reception teachers working with 4-year-olds also need reminding that a 4-year-old does not 'have to go to assembly' – he or she does not even have to go to school!

Alongside their role as advocates of nursery education and of very young children, teachers also need to take into account national education legislation – even though it often does not explicitly apply to them. The 1988 Education Reform Act – in particular the National Curriculum – does not directly involve children under 5. Nursery teachers apparently have a choice – they can either ignore it or decide for themselves how it applies to them. But have they actually got a choice? Even though the National Curriculum is intended to cover the 5–16 age range, a document published by the National Curriculum Council (1989) has a section headed 'The Education of Children Under Five' which links attainment targets with activities and experiences undertaken by under-5s in nursery and reception classes, and in many primary schools nursery staff are being expected to adapt to the changes alongside their colleagues.

To many teachers their 'choice' is clear. If they want to survive, they must be seen to be operating as part of mainstream education. When annual reports to governors were introduced, nursery schools, which were not included in the legislation, were exempt, but many headteachers decided to comply with the regulation because they did not want parents or colleagues to feel they were running a less serious establishment – and in any case encouraging parents to attend a meeting at school is often less difficult because of the close relationships already being developed.

However, operating as part of mainstream has its disadvantages, as we have already seen, and nursery class teachers complain that their greater involvement in the primary school sometimes leads to unrealistic and inapproriate demands being made on them (as described in Chapter 4). It is worth reiterating that, for the sake of the children, teachers must keep sight of the principles which underpin their work, if they are to work in co-operation with primary colleagues in ways which do not force them to compromise their beliefs.

Recent developments in education have stretched all teachers to the limit, but nursery teachers, because of their position on the fringes of the changes, have been involved in a considerable amount of soul-searching. Experienced teachers who are confident in their knowledge and skills have been able to adapt their approach to take account of changes in school, and of the need for greater accountability. For example, one teacher explained to colleagues on a course how she had resisted a request to produce plans for themes for a year because she considered this to be inappropriate, but offered alternative, long-term plans which would show how the provision and experiences she intended to offer could cover all curriculum areas at a variety of levels. Being able to offer acceptable, meaningful alternatives to inappropriate requests is a skill increasingly required by nursery class teachers working for headteachers who have little or no early years experience. Many headteachers are looking to their nursery staff for this kind of guidance – if it is not forthcoming they have little alternative but to insist on an approach, however unsuitable that may be.

Looking Outwards and Inwards

The developments briefly outlined above, in conjunction with the research evidence referred to in previous chapters, have transformed nursery education. They have certainly resulted in many teachers adopting a more rigorous, analytical approach. Timothy Raison (then chair of ESAC) when speaking to a group of researchers at the National Children's Bureau in 1989, commented on the developments he had observed on his recent visits to nursery schools and classes compared with visits made ten years previously. He commented on the greater rigour involved, particularly in relation to recordkeeping.

These improvements have been possible because teachers have looked outward to refresh their view of education and society, and have then tested out their own attitudes and practice against the new evidence. They have also looked inside themselves to try to identify their own outmoded ideas and prejudices. At times when political initiatives seem to clash with principles or with the children's needs, they have worked together to try to find an appropriate way forward.

On the whole, they have not been well supported to cope with change – particularly the kinds of developments with which they have recently had to deal. Teachers often complain that courses specifically for nursery staff are uncommon. Although they value courses which also involve primary colleagues, they feel they also need time to discuss specific nursery concerns. When they are organized, nursery courses are invariably oversubscribed. Teachers attend for a variety of reasons, the most important of which is often the opportunities provided for discussion with colleagues – it is nearly always difficult to bring a course to an end because teachers continue chatting (about their work) long after the course has officially finished (Lally, 1989a). Their enthusiasm for, and commitment to, their work is apparent. So is their concern to do the job better – hopefully some of the ways in which they express this enthusiasm, commitment and concern have been transmitted in earlier chapters. When they are able to attend courses, it is this willingness to analyse themselves which makes work with groups of nursery teachers so rewarding.

Nursery teachers are their own worst critics – in fact, the most effective teachers find more to worry about than those who really need to examine their practice or attitudes. This is probably because, the more questions we ask in relation to ourselves, and in relation to the society in which we live, the more subsequent questions we generate and the less certain we are that there are any answers let alone definitive ones. Those adults who want or need to be involved with certainty, are unlikely to make effective teachers of any age group. Very young children need and deserve adults who are prepared to set out on a voyage of discovery with them.

Training for Personal Responsibility

Initial and in-service courses which emphasize the analysis of attitudes, situations and problems validate teachers' concerns. The old 'tips for teachers' transmission model of training where the tutor offered ideas for activities for teachers to copy in school, is no longer seen to be appropriate, although some teachers, who have understandably become anxious as a result of the pace of change, still say they want to be told what to do. For these teachers the process of thinking issues through for themselves is a difficult one, and they seem to want someone else to tell them what to think.

These teachers have not accepted personal responsibility for their teaching. They have not realized (or do not wish to acknowledge) that they carry ultimate responsibility for what happens in their class. Nor are they recognizing that they have choices to make, preferring to delude themselves with the idea that others determine what they have to do – 'the headteacher has told me to do this' or 'the parents wouldn't like it if I did that'. There are always some restraints on what we can and cannot do in a particular situation, but there are also choices. We can choose how we organize furniture, resources and time, we can choose whether or not we share our principles and the reasons for them with others, and we can choose which experiences we involve ourselves with. These are only some of the choices – others are to be found in other chapters if we care to look for them. Using others as an excuse (or blaming them) is an effective way of avoiding responsibility – an effective way of preventing ourselves from having to confront an issue. It is also an effective way of forgetting or ignoring the needs of young children.

The effective nursery teacher is characterized by her unswerving commitment to young children and their families. She attends courses because she wants the chance to analyse in more depth, in the company of colleagues, some of the concerns which are foremost in her mind. She does not expect answers – instead she hopes for greater clarity or, perhaps, a deeper insight into the issue, and expects to gain support from realizing that she is not alone. Above all, she gains strength from discussions with others. In the words of one teacher at the end of a course:

> I think it [the course] has made me realize how important it is to work with people who have been trained and with whom I share common methods, because of how difficult it is to get across nursery ethos . . . the course has helped me crystallize ideas which are more important than others.

Similar words are written on many course evaluation forms. They highlight the commitment of the teacher to gain the support she needs to help her with the difficult task of sharing her ideas with others. Complexity is never easy to explain, but these teachers know that for the sake of the children they have a responsibility to try. They know how easy it is to be diverted from their own priorities and feel the need to get together regularly with like-minded practitioners to revitalize themselves and retain the courage of their convictions. This is particularly important for those working in classes attached to primary schools. They, in particular, need the support gained from sharing and articulating concerns with others which is 'so essential for sustaining enthusiastic and lively classroom practice' (Osborn and Milbank, 1987, p. 219).

This does not mean that in-service training should be left to the group. Courses, which involve unstructured group work and offer little in the way of stimuli or ideas for teachers to consider, are nearly always unsatisfactory. In fact, it is possible to apply some of the principles of early childhood education to in-service education. In-service courses should:

- Be directly relevant to the concerns of those taking part (whenever possible participants should be involved in planning the course content).
- Draw directly on and build on the experience of the group.

- Provide a supportive environment where all participants have the chance to contribute and share ideas.
- Enable group members to operate at different levels of understanding.
- Acknowledge achievements to date and help group members to identify for themselves the next step in their learning.
- Question assumptions and encourage the group members to question themselves.
- Offer a framework for tackling complex issues or problems.
- Encourage participants to write their thoughts down, since the process of writing often leads to greater clarity.
- Draw together the salient points from all discussions and make connections between them.

In-service courses should demonstrate recognition of achievements, while at the same time inspire teachers to continue to seek for improvement. There is clearly a delicate balance here. It is easy to demoralize teachers, or to encourage them so much they believe they have found all the answers. On any course some teachers will feel more insecure than others, and it is the course tutor's responsibility to find out about individuals by observing and listening, and to offer an appropriate balance of reassurance and challenge to each one. The longer the course, the more possible it is to get this balance right. Perhaps this is why the advisory teacher model of in-service support is a useful one. Through working alongside an individual teacher and her team, it is possible to match the support offered directly to specific needs. It also involves trainers or advisers in confronting head on the very real issues faced by particular teams, and offers an extension of the partnership approach to learning advocated in earlier chapters.

Teachers as Agents of Change

Throughout this book we have seen how teachers have developed their own practice in order to respond more effectively to the needs of young children and their families. These developments were summarized by some experienced inner London teachers during a course when they were asked to say how they and their practice had changed since they started to work with young children. They highlighted the following areas of development, many of which were felt to be ongoing concerns:

1. *Teamwork.* The teachers felt there was a greater emphasis on a whole team approach with all team members sharing in policy-making and often in training. Their role as team leader had been highlighted.

2. *Organization of the learning environment.* Workshop areas, where children have easy access to resources and can work autonomously, have been developed. This way of organizing has led to staff re-assessing their role, and in some cases raising their expectations of children.

3. *Equal opportunities.* There is now a greater awareness of the need to take a critical look at provision and attitudes. Equal opportunities policies have been developed as a result of a growing awareness of the need to prevent discrimination (on the grounds of culture, gender, class and special educational needs) from limiting children's opportunities. Specifically, bilingualism is now more likely to be seen as an asset (rather than as a problem) as a result of in-service training and the work of bilingual support teachers (the inner London based Bilingual Under Fives team was felt to have had a very positive effect on attitudes and practice).

4. *Attitudes to parents are felt to be more positive.* The teachers felt that, through increased contact with families, they had come to respect and value the parents' intimate knowledge of their children and had recognized the need to strive for a more equal partnership. Initiatives such as home visiting, shared recordkeeping, involvement of parents in the curriculum (both working in the class, and taking part in teacher-led explanatory workshops), toddler groups, parents rooms, and toy and book lending libraries, were all given as examples of the increased commitment to involve the whole family in nursery education.

5. *Links with other agencies* have developed out of a concern for the development of the 'whole child'. Work with speech therapists, health visitors, educational psychologists and social services staff is developing into more of a partnership as teachers have recognized the need to share expertise.

6. *Personality development.* Many of the teachers felt they had changed personally as a result of their teaching experience. Through working with nursery nurses some felt they had become more sensitive to children's social and emotional needs, and others felt they were now more able to help children establish boundaries and negotiate. (Perhaps these are two issues for initial trainers to consider, since they are too important to be left to chance.)

7. *The curriculum.* The teaching of some subject areas has developed to take into account research evidence and the requirements of the National Curriculum. The teachers were particularly excited by the developmental approach to reading and writing which recent research has inspired, because it fits well with and extends their idea of the learning process. Above all, this approach finally puts to rest the notion that there is such a thing as a pre-reading or pre-writing activity, and

re-defines effective nursery practice in terms of early reading and writing experiences. Many teachers are tired of the 'pre-' prefix (as in preschool, etc.) feeling it devalues everything they do. Science and technology teaching has also developed, as nursery teachers have become more aware, through reading the National Curriculum documents, of what can be learnt by young children. Outdoor experience is generally felt to be more highly valued with teachers trying to ensure it reflects more closely, and offers the same breadth of experience as, the provision made indoors.

8. *Recordkeeping.* Methods have been evolving in the ways described in Chapter 4, and are being influenced by the National Curriculum as teachers attempt to note relevant attainment.

9. *Continuity.* The teachers feel they have worked hard to ensure that children transfer from home to nursery class smoothly, and are concerned to ensure that the transition from nursery to infant class is equally stress free. In particular, they are concerned that skills children have developed at nursery should be acknowledged and built on in the reception class. Links between nursery and infant teachers are developing, but some nursery teachers feel they are making all the effort!

This list of changes is a testimony to the commitment of nursery teachers. Many of these initiatives are at the forefront of educational development. For example, in their evidence to the Education, Science and Arts Committee, the Tutors for Advanced Courses for Teachers of Young Children (TACTYC) made the point that 'early years teachers are probably among the best in terms of the assessment procedures, the profiling and the monitoring of young children at the present time' (ESAC, 1988). They are in a strong position to take a lead both in whole school and local authority initiatives.

The introduction of the National Curriculum, with its emphasis on continuity of experience, has provided teachers with an opportunity to argue for the 'bottom up' model of education they have always wanted. Instead of feeling they are under pressure to teach 'to specific but limited targets' (Clark, 1988), they have the chance to describe to colleagues the children's achievements in the nursery and explain how these relate to the programmes of study. Infant teachers will need this information if they are to ensure continuity of experience and progression in learning. Where nursery and infant teachers work together at courses or staff meetings, it is possible for them to share ideas and to find ways of working towards the same objectives even though there are fundamental differences in resourcing and staffing ratios. With mutual understanding and respect, both groups of teachers can gain support and strength from working together in this way.

There is scope then for teachers to increase their influence within the primary sector. It is not yet easy for them to do so. When asked how they will share ideas discussed on courses with colleagues, nursery class teachers often make it clear that it is difficult for them to have any influence. Comments such as 'I'm regarded as a separate issue in the nursery – staff won't address my issues' (Lally, 1989a) are not at all uncommon. How much this is due to a real lack of interest on the part of primary teachers or to a feeling that nursery practice is different and therefore irrelevant, and how much it is a reflection of a lack of confidence on the part of nursery teachers, is not entirely clear. What is apparent, though, is the isolation and low status felt by most nursery staff – they often feel they are marginalized or even patronized by colleagues.

Time is also an issue. In a climate of unrelenting change it is not surprising that there is no time for sharing of the kind being advocated. Staff meetings seem to be increasingly taken up with issues of accountability – how to demonstrate curriculum coverage in the simplest possible way – at the expense of a discussion of underlying concerns, such as whether one style of recording is appropriate for the whole school. There are signs that where in-service training is available, nursery teachers are gaining the confidence to question and to offer alternative ways of looking at a particular issue. For the sake of the children in their classes, and in the interests of the school as a whole, they must be encouraged further by headteachers to contribute in this way.

Raising the Status of Teachers

The suggestion that incentive allowances could be offered to nursery teachers in order to raise their status (ESAC, 1989) has been acted upon in some schools and local authorities. Under the previous salary system, scale 2 posts were often held by teachers in charge of double nursery units, but these extra payments disappeared when all scale 1 and 2 posts were incorporated in the Main Professional Grade. Although this was meant to imply that all teachers had the chance to receive a scale 2 salary, many teachers felt that they had been particularly badly affected – the limited number of new incentive allowances seemed out of reach in a primary school with competing priorities. The ESAC recommendation was therefore enthusiastically welcomed.

Some teachers have received an allowance in recognition of the responsibilities involved in running the nursery class. In these cases, the extra commitment to community links, team leadership and the provision of a sound foundation for learning has been acknowledged. Other teachers have taken on extra responsibilities, such as a subject area, or an issue, for example, continuity across the early years.

These responsibilities almost always involve dissemination within the school, and sometimes within a local authority. It is here that the teacher has been given the chance to raise her own status. Through demonstrating her skills to others, whether in relation to community work, shared record-keeping, science, language or maths, she has the opportunity to show her professionalism – to make it clear that nursery teaching is not a soft option. If she is also able to help others understand her philosophy or use some of her ideas to improve their practice, she can also command their respect.

Many of the skills involved in nursery teaching are directly transferable to work with adults. Adults respond to warmth and enthusiasm, patience and interest, just as children do. They also respond best to someone who facilitates their learning and does not tell them what to do. Sadly, some teachers lack confidence in their own ability and need support if they are to reach their full potential in this area. Some local education authorities, such as Suffolk, Newham, and Sutton, have recognized this need and have offered training in group work skills to experienced nursery teachers to enable them to contribute more confidently to in-service initiatives, both in their own schools and in the authority as a whole – sometimes involving under-5s' workers from social services and the voluntary sector.

All of these developments offer real chances for teachers to take a more prominent role within and outside their own school. Many have been keen to gain the recognition they believe they deserve and have responded enthusiastically. It is particularly important at a time when there is a shortage of nursery trained teachers, and when some colleges have no nursery trained tutors, that those with appropriate training and experience are actively encouraged to share their expertise. This encouragement involves reassuring teachers that they will be given time to take on this extra responsibility, and that the children will not suffer while they are doing other things. Whether or not this kind of encouragement can be given at the present time of scarce resources is debatable. It is very likely that teachers will not wish to undertake any activity which negatively affects the experience of the children in their class. Young children are too vulnerable to be passed from person to person, and unless satisfactory cover arrangements can be made, many teachers will wish to remain in their classes. Chatting to nursery teachers at the beginning of daytime courses (if they are lucky enough to be able to attend one) quickly reveals their concern for the children they have left behind.

There has been no intention in this chapter to imply that nursery teachers care more, or are more committed than other teachers. This could not be substantiated. However, it is possible to suggest that involvement in nursery education exposes teachers to children at a very vulnerable stage in their development, and requires them to be concerned about whole families and communities in a way less likely to be required of teachers of older children. It is this involvement which inspires the commitment and enthusiasm, and also the self-evaluation described in this chapter. Contact with parents and children from a variety of social and cultural backgrounds heightens the teacher's awareness of some of the inadequacies of the education system, and prevents her from becoming complacent.

Often, the nursery teacher's reluctance to talk in glowing terms about her work is a result of the very real humility which develops when one becomes aware of one's own inadequacy to deal with the concerns of some families. It is also a result of her awareness of her role as a partner (with parents and children) in the education process. Such close involvement with the community can lead to feelings of despair. It is to the credit of the teacher that she usually retains hope, and concentrates on doing the best she possibly can.

Some Points for Discussion

Personal Development

- How has your understanding of and attitudes towards society and people changed since you became a nursery teacher?
- Has your view of the role of the teacher changed?
- What is responsible for these changes?
- How have you made yourself and your team members aware of them?
- How has your practice been affected?

The Children's Background

- How much do you know about the backgrounds of the children you teach?
- How are these different from your own background?
- What steps have you taken to make yourself aware of your own stereotyped attitudes towards childrearing practices, cultural backgrounds and religious beliefs, the role of women, etc.?
- How have you tried to see things from the point of view of the families you work with?

- Can you remember anything you have done or said which revealed your own prejudice?

Teacher as Campaigner

- To what extent have you seen your role as a campaigning one?
- Are the families you work with aware of the discretionary nature of nursery education?
- What can you do both individually, and with other nursery teachers in your area, to help others understand more about nursery education?
- How do you view new developments in education?
- Do you feel that your firm principles enable you to interpret new initiatives, such as the National Curriculum, in ways which are consistent with the needs of the children, or do you feel pressured to work in inappropriate ways?
- How could you and your team (including parents) learn together about new developments?

Influencing Colleagues

- What opportunities have you initiated or accepted to explain your work to primary colleagues?
- What additional opportunities could you make both in your own school and in the local authority?
- What are your strengths as a teacher?
- What do you feel you particularly have to offer colleagues?
- How could you anticipate and equip yourself to deal with difficult questions or comments such as 'Why don't you sit them down to do some real work?'
- How could you gain support and confidence from nursery colleagues?

7

ONGOING ISSUES AND CONCERNS

This book has emphasized the climate of change within which the nursery teacher operates, and the ways in which she adapts her approach to take educational developments and changes in society into account. In this final chapter, we will look briefly at some of the issues which are likely to continue to concern her.

A number of words have become associated with 'good practice'. These words are liberally used by those discussing provision for 3- and 4-year-olds – some of them are to be found earlier in this book. When listening to these words being used, and thinking about the provision or practice they are describing, it is striking how little unanimity there is in relation to their meanings. Many of the words have never been defined in the nursery context and, consequently, each person who uses them is able to apply his or her own definition. Discussions with teachers reveal that they are confused by the use of some of the words, and are looking for a more open debate of the issues they raise, which are often concealed or ignored. Above all, they want to challenge some of the assumptions implied by current uses of these words.

In this chapter, we will take a look at some of these issues and assumptions – not with a view to reaching a final definition of the words, but to encourage a proper debate of the complexity involved in what are apparently simple ideas. This debate is essential if services for young children are to develop in a properly considered way. It is also important that teachers have the opportunity to make their views known and that, when offered this chance, they are able to grasp it. Like everyone else involved, they need to have thought through the issues for themselves, and identified how they might be, or would like to be, affected.

Co-ordination

This word has been in use for many years now in relation to services for under-5s (Pugh, 1988). Co-ordination is generally considered to be 'a good thing' and yet there has been little real progress. This is possibly because there has been no comprehensive attempt, either nationally or locally, to answer two crucial questions:

1. What is meant by 'co-ordination' and what would it involve in practice?
2. What is it hoped to achieve by co-ordinating services for under-5s?

These questions are, of course, considerably easier to address in situations where provision is plentiful. It is no coincidence that those local authorities which are moving towards co-ordination of services, such as Strathclyde, Manchester and Islington, are those which have above average amounts of provision. It is obviously easier to co-ordinate a lot than a little. In fact, some cynics believe that co-ordination is actually about making a little look like a lot.

A further question which needs to be asked is: when is it an appropriate time to talk about co-ordination? Is the most appropriate time a time when there are low levels of statutory provision, when parents are despairing of ever finding something suitable for their child, and when under-5s' workers feel threatened by real and anticipated cutbacks?

What appears to happen when provision is limited and vulnerable to cuts, is a lowering of morale amongst workers in all types of provision. Workers become defensive and protective of their own provision, and may even criticize others to make their own provision seem more attractive. Are these the circumstances in which to ask workers to co-operate with others? If not, what would be the right circumstances? How could a more positive climate be created? Sadly, these are questions which policy-makers sometimes forget to address. Any change requires careful ground-work to be undertaken, and yet nursery workers often feel they are the last to be considered.

In the absence of real consultation or explanation, workers are left to jump to their own conclusions about motives. It is not surprising that many teachers see co-ordination as a merging of provision, or that they fear that this merging will lead to a drop in educational standards. They also worry that they will be separated from the rest of the education system, and that their status and career prospects will be damaged. They have not been reassured that co-ordination will retain the strengths of existing provision, and allow those strengths to flourish, since this would be expensive, and the chances of extra resources being made available seem slim.

The way forward here is clearly for policy-makers to listen to those working with young children and for workers from statutory and voluntary provision to be given opportunities to discuss together their hopes and fears. Whatever we finally decide co-ordination means, it, like any other initiative, will only work if the goodwill of the workforce is retained, and if they are helped to see each other as allies rather than enemies. Clearly, when parents are looking for full-day, all-year-round care and education for their children, teachers need to consider the relevance of sessional, part-time nursery education, and be prepared to suggest alternative ways forward.

Partnership

A second, closely linked word, is partnership. Teachers are expected to work in partnership with children, parents and with others working with young children, and many use this word to describe relationships they are involved in. Attempts at definitions of this word have been made, often with the aim of helping workers realize what is involved in the concept of partnership. Pugh and De'Ath (1989, p. 33) define partnership as: 'a working relationship that is characterised by a shared sense of purpose, mutual respect and the willingness to negotiate. This implies a sharing of information, responsibility, skills, decision-making and accountability'. In earlier chapters we have seen how teachers are moving towards a partnership approach with children, parents and other workers. However, many of them are realizing the dilemmas involved. Some of the parents they work with do not share their values or sense of purpose. What kind of partnership is it possible to develop with a staunch supporter of the National Front when you are committed to developing an anti-racist policy? How do you share information with someone whose language you do not speak, when there is no interpreter or translator available? And, more fundamentally, how can decision-making really be shared when you are ultimately accountable?

These are real and very worrying issues for the nursery teacher. She is aware that her professional responsibilities sometimes get in the way of the kind of partnership described above. There are times when she has to assert her authority in the interests of the school or class. There is little doubt that many teachers have developed more flexible and open ways of working with children and parents, but, as they have done so, they have recognized that a partnership as defined above may not always be possible or even desirable.

It is encouraging to listen to teachers facing their concerns honestly. What they have achieved is often much nearer to a partnership than teachers of older children or other under-5s' workers have managed, and yet they are aware of the constraints. Perhaps individual teachers should be encouraged to define their own relationship with parents. Relationships will inevitably vary according to staffing ratios and school ethos, and will be affected by the parent's ability to choose a particular type of provision for their child (the choices open to parents will be discussed in the next section). Teachers need to take an honest look at the relationships they have established, recognizing their own limitations as well as the needs of the families they work with. Only from a basis of honesty is it possible to develop effectively these relationships.

Partnership with other under-5s' workers has been less easy to achieve given a history of suspicion and, sometimes, jealousy between the different groups. Teachers, through the professional barriers they sometimes erect, may alienate other workers (Watt, 1977), and other workers may be resentful of the status afforded to the qualified teacher. The central questions here seem to be: are under-5s' workers able to accept that they have different but complementary experience and skills, and can they accept that they have something to learn from each other?

Sometimes teachers overcompensate and in trying to avoid being seen as 'the professional' they denigrate their own training and experience. At one multi-disciplinary conference a teacher was heard to comment that her training had taught her nothing, and that she felt she had a lot to learn from the playgroup leaders present. This is as unhelpful as the remark made by a playgroup leader who, when a teacher shared her planning records with the group, said smugly, 'Of course, I do all that in my head'! This example shows the difficulties involved in working respectfully with others from different backgrounds.

Some local authorities have tried to address these problems through multi-disciplinary training courses involving workers from statutory and voluntary provision. Given the climate (outlined above) within which these courses operate, and the different levels of understanding of those involved, it is not surprising that they are not always successful. Sometimes relationships deteriorate during a course as group members struggle to communicate with each other, and professional jealousies come to the surface. Once again it seems important that some groundwork is undertaken before bringing people together in this way.

In some areas, local groups have been established to enable workers across the statutory and voluntary sectors to meet each other. In providing a forum for informal discussion, these groups are extremely valuable. They have given workers a chance to gain a deeper understanding of each others' roles and perspectives. Because they are often a grassroots initiative, they are well supported and have the potential to break down barriers and to inspire a collaborative approach. Some of these informal groups have decided to ask for or to organize their own training sessions on topics of mutual interest. This seems to be a more productive approach to multi-disciplinary training, and again it demands that workers themselves have some choice and control.

Choice

This word has been used on a number of occasions in earlier chapters. It is regularly used by government when they emphasize the need for parents to have a choice of provision. There are three main areas of choice which the nursery teacher concerns herself with.

Choice of Provision for Children

If we accept that having a choice involves being offered alternatives to choose from, we also have to admit that there is very little choice of provision for young children in Britain. In many areas there is no nursery education, and those parents who want full-day care find they also need a high salary, since this provision is usually only available to those who can pay for the service. The reality for most parents is, therefore, an acceptance of whatever (if anything) happens to be available in their neighbourhood.

This is regrettable, since some parents out of sheer desperation, are accepting provision which they should probably not be accepting. In an ideal world parents would make informed choices between different types of provision offering different philosophies and practice. It would be up to workers to explain what they were offering, and to encourage parents to select the provision which best met their expectations and their child's needs. In areas where this ideal world is almost a reality (that is, those areas where statutory, voluntary and private provision is plentiful), parents become more selective, and are more likely to look at, and ask questions about, all the establishments on offer before making a final choice. Nevertheless, in my own experience of working in such an area, the only parents with a total choice are those with the money to pay if they choose to do so. It is clear though that, where parents are able to exercise their right to choose, staff in all types of provision need to clarify what they are offering and why. This must surely improve the quality of all provision, since, if they are not asked to explain and account for their practice, there is the risk that workers become complacent. A central question here is: will we ever have high quality provision without choice?

Nursery teachers would like to feel that parents opting for their class are doing so because they believe it offers their child the kind of education they want. This is why they take the time to explain their philosophy and practice. They know that, until all parents have a real choice, teachers cannot be sure that those bringing their children to their classes are doing so because they share the school's underlying philosophy. Discussions with parents during the child's time in the nursery class often reveal fundamental disagreements which, as we saw earlier, put into question the whole concept of a partnership based on a shared sense of purpose. These issues will only be resolved when provision is increased and all families with children under the age of 5 have the chance to choose.

Choice for Children within Provision

The need to offer children the chance to make choices in relation to their own learning was discussed in Chapter 3. We also considered the difficulties facing staff who had been more used to controlling children. Teachers must continue to ask themselves critically whether they are trusting children enough, and whether they could offer more choice.

These questions are particularly important at a time of educational change. We have seen how teachers are feeling pressured by the National Curriculum. One teacher commented during an in-service session 'I feel as if I'm chasing attainment targets', and went on to explain that she felt she was being expected by the rest of her school to work in ways which undermined recent developments in nursery education.

The time has come for nursery teachers to replace the 'top down' model they have lived with for so long with a 'bottom up' model which offers real hope for the education of all children, not just 3- and 4-year-olds. This has already happened in some primary schools with top junior classes working to the same child-centred philosophy as the nursery class.

If nursery teachers can see the National Curriculum as an initiative which has in some ways broadened our view of the curriculum (through its emphasis on the range of knowledge and skills to be learnt), and in other ways narrowed it (because it devalues personal and social development and the creative arts – both so important in nursery education), they should be able to work their way through the dilemmas. It would be a tragedy if the National Curriculum were to limit choice, since there is no need for this to happen. If teachers get to know children, they place themselves in a strong position to help them broaden the scope of the choices they make. Surely the aim of all educators must be to encourage children to choose to learn. Nursery teachers have been examining the implications of this aim and wish to continue to develop their practice. They need to have their arguments ready if they are to resist the pressures.

Choice for Staff in Relation to Practice

Everyone involved in training nursery teachers has to take into account the issue of confidence. What is the best way of helping teachers develop the confidence to make and defend their own choices? In the previous chapter we saw how teachers sometimes try to avoid taking responsibility by blaming others, and are sometimes unable to see that they have any choice.

Pressures caused by the hurried introduction of new educational initiatives have compounded these feelings of helplessness. In a world where it seems as if we are all told what to do, it is difficult to see any options available to us, and yet, in their own classes, teachers have a considerable amount of autonomy. In earlier chapters we have seen how teachers have a responsibility to choose (with the help of research evidence) the principles which underpin their work, and how they translate these principles into practice.

Firm principles, which can be explained with reference to evidence, make the task of articulating nursery education to others considerably easier. They also make it possible to question some of the less appropriate demands made on teachers. Helping teachers develop their own set of principles is an important responsibility of all trainers. Without them teachers are vulnerable. Trainers at initial and in-service level also need to encourage teachers to apply their principles to practice since there is sometimes inconsistency between what teachers say they believe in, and what they actually do. When teachers can clearly articulate the relationship between principles and practice, they become strong advocates of their profession and of young children. It is to be hoped that all teachers will choose to act as advocates in this way. Teachers need to remember that the young child is affected by the choices they make, and need to ask themselves: out of the alternatives available to me, have I chosen the course of action which is in the best interests of the children?

Equality

This word, or its implications, has featured throughout this book. It is repeated again to emphasize the considerable amount of work still to be done if we are to ensure that all children have the opportunity to reach their full potential, and are not limited by racism, sexism and attitudes to class or special educational needs. Many teachers are aware that writing an equal opportunities policy is only one step. Ensuring that this policy is consistently put into practice is a much harder task, since it involves tackling attitudes, both of those in school and of those in the wider community, as we saw in Chapter 2.

Schools are a part of society and as such reflect the values and attitudes of that society. Menter (1989, p. 95) describes five 'social institutions which shape everyone's experience – the state, the media, the community, the home, the school'. In other words, school is only one influence in children's lives. This can lead teachers to become despondent – to feel that there is no point in trying to do anything. This is obviously unacceptable if we believe that education can contribute to all-round personal development.

Teachers have a responsibility to broaden their own view of society, and acknowledge the inequalities which exist both outside and within school. Having begun to do this they can then begin the process of working with others – colleagues, children and parents – to ensure that all children are positively encouraged.

Teachers cannot change society but they can make a contribution to the change process. When it all seems too difficult, teachers need to ask themselves: would I want this treatment for my child?

Time

All of the intitiatives described in this book have time implications. Time is something which teachers say they do not have. It therefore seems appropriate to end this book with a request to headteachers and policy-makers.

Nursery teachers have often been at the forefront of educational change. They have developed their practice without the benefit of non-contact time or, in many cases, even without a full lunch break. They have done so willingly and enthusiastically because they care about the children and want to know more about them. Work with parents and the community often has to be undertaken outside of school hours, since staffing ratios are rarley generous enough to permit any other arrangement. Recordkeeping of the kind described in Chapter 4 often involves hours of work at home as well as the discussions with colleagues which take place before and after school.

Nursery teachers have quite rightly been praised for their achievements, and have been encouraged to develop their work further. If they are not to become discouraged, they need to see that the commitment involved has been acknowledged. More than anything else they would like some (however little) cover during the school day to enable them to consolidate and develop their ideas further. In the absence of this support, it is possible that the goodwill they have shown to date will diminish.

If we really recognize the expertise of the nursery teacher (as opposed to paying lip-service to her skills) the moment has come to reward her with that most precious commodity – time. The rewards for the school will be measured in terms of parental commitment and firm foundations for children's learning. They may even be greater, for, if the teacher can initiate and achieve what she has so far without this extra time, it is certain that with it she will initiate and achieve even more.

REFERENCES

Asher, S. R., Renshaw, P. D. and Hymel, S. (1982) Peer Relations and the Development of Social Skills, in S. Moore and C. Cooper (eds.) *The Young Child: Reviews of Research*, Vol. 3, National Association for the Education of Young Children, Washington DC.

Athey, C. (1990) *Extending Thought in Young Children: A Parent–Teacher Partnership*, Paul Chapman, London.

BAECE (1990) *Nursery Schools: A View from Within*, BAECE, London.

Barrett, G. (1986) *Starting School: An Evaluation of the Experience*, AMMA/UEA, Norwich.

Barrs, M., Ellis, S., Hester, H. and Thomas, A. (1988) *The Primary Language Record Handbook*, ILEA/CLPE, London.

Bennett, N. and Kell, J. (1989) *A Good Start? Four Year Olds in Infant Schools*, Blackwell, Oxford.

Berenstain, S. (1981) *Bears in the Night*, Collins, London.

Blatchford, P., Battle, S. and Mays, J. (1982) *The First Transition: Home to Preschool*, NFER/Nelson, Windsor.

Blenkin, G. M. and Kelly, A. V. (eds.) (1987) *Early Childhood Education: A Developmental Curriculum*, Paul Chapman, London.

Blenkin, G. M. and Whitehead, M. R. (1987) Creating a Context for Development, in G. M. Blenkin and A. V. Kelly (eds.) op. cit., pp. 32–60.

Bone, M. (1977) *Preschool Children and the Need for Daycare*, DHSS survey, HMSO, London.

Brierley, J. (1984) *A Human Birthright: Giving the Young Brain a Chance*, BAECE, London.

Briggs, R. (1978) *The Snowman*, Hamish Hamilton, London.

Broom, J. (1990) *Young Children Using Computers*, BAECE, London.

Bruce, T. (1987) *Early Childhood Education*, Hodder & Stoughton, London.

Clark, M. M. (1988) *Children Under Five: Educational Research and Evidence*, Gordon & Breach, London.

Clift, P., Cleave, S. and Griffin, M. (1980) *The Aims, Role and Deployment of Staff in the Nursery*, NFER/Nelson, Windsor.

CRE (1977) *Caring for Under Fives in a Multi-Racial Society*, CRE, London.

CRE (1990) *From Cradle to School. A Practical Guide to Race Equality and Childcare*, CRE, London.

David, T. (1990) *Under Five – Under Educated?*, Open University Press, Milton Keynes.

Derman-Sparks, L. and the ABC Task Force (1989) *Anti-Bias Curriculum. Tools for Empowering Young Children*, National Association for the Education of Young Children, Washington DC.

DES (1972) *Education: A Framework for Expansion*, HMSO, London.

DES (1983) *Teaching Quality*, HMSO, London.

DES (1989a) *Aspects of Primary Education: The Education of Children Under Five*, HMSO, London.

DES (1989b) *Educational Provision for the under Fives. Observations by the Government and Local Authority Associations on the First Report of the Committee in Session 1988-89*, HMSO, London.

DES (1990) *Starting with Quality*, HMSO, London.

Donaldson, M. (1978) *Children's Minds*, Fontana, Glasgow.

Dowling, M. (1988) *Education 3 to 5: A Teachers' Handbook*, Paul Chapman, London.

Drummond, M. J., Lally, M. and Pugh, G. (1989) *Working with Children: Developing a Curriculum for the Early Years*, NCB/Nottingham Educational Supplies, Nottingham.

ESAC (1988) *Educational Provision for the Under Fives*, Vol. II, Minutes of Evidence and Appendices, HMSO, London.

ESAC (1989) *Educational Provision for the Under Fives*, HMSO, London.

EYCG (1989) *Early childhood Education. The Early Years Curriculum and the National Curriculum*, Trentham Books, Stoke-on-Trent.

Family Policy Studies Centre (1990) *Family Change and Future Policy*, Joseph Rowntree Trust, London.

Fletcher, D. (1988) Future Heart Problems Seen in 3-year-olds, in *The Daily Telegraph*, 12 May.

Hazareesingh, S., Simms, K. and Anderson, P. (1989) *Educating the Whole Child. A Holistic Approach to Education in Early Years*, Building Blocks, London.

Hill, E. (1980) *Where's Spot?*, Heinemann, London.

Holt, J. (1970) *How Children Learn*, Penguin, Harmondsworth.

Hughes, M. (1986) *Children and Number*, Blackwell, Oxford.

Hurst, V. (1987) Parents and Professionals: Partnership in Early Childhood Education, in G. M. Blenkin and A. V. Kelly (eds.) op. cit., pp. 94–110.

Hurst, V. (1991) *Planning for Early Learning: the Education of the Under Fives*, Paul Chapman, London.

Industrial Society (1969) *The Manager as Leader*, The Industrial Society, London.

Ironbridge Gorge Museum (1989) *Under Fives and Museums. Guidelines for Teachers*, Ironbridge Gorge Museum, Telford.

Isaacs, S. (1954) *The Educational Value of the Nursery School*, BAECE, London.

Katz, L. and Chard, S. (1989) *Engaging Children's Minds. The Project Approach*, Ablex Publishing Corporation, Norwood, New Jersey.

Laishley, J. (1987) *Working with Young Children: A Handbook* (2nd edn), Edward Arnold, London.

Lally, M. (1986) Setting up an Anti-sexist Nursery, in C. Adams (ed.) *Primary Matters*, ILEA, London.

Lally, M. (1989a) *An Integrated Approach to the National Curriculum in the Early Years 3–7*, National Children's Bureau, London.

Lally, M. (1989b) *Curriculum for Three to Five Year Olds*, Highlight No. 89, National Children's Bureau, London.

Lazar, I. and Darlington, R. (1982) Lasting Effects of Early Education: a Report from the Consortium for Longitudinal Studies, *Monographs of the Society for Research in Child Development*, Serial No. 195, Volume 47.

Menter, I. (1989) 'They're too Young to Notice': Young Children and Racism, in G. Barrett (ed.) *Disaffection from School? The Early Years*, Falmer Press, Lewes, pp. 91–104.

Metz, M. (1987) The Development of Mathematical Understanding, in G. M. Blenkin and A. V. Kelly (eds.) op. cit., pp. 84–201.

Milner, D. (1975) *Children and Race*, Penguin, Harmondsworth.

Milner, D. (1983) *Children and Race – Ten Years On*, Ward Lock, London.

Moyles, J. (1989) *Just Playing? The Role and Status of Play in Early Childhood Education*, Open University Press, Milton Keynes.

National Curriculum Council (1989) *A Framework for the Primary Curriculum*, NCC, York.

NFER/SCDC (1987) *Four Year Olds in School: Policy and Practice*, A Seminar Report, NFER/SCDC.

NSPCC (1990) Sad Indication, *Children's Friend*, Issue No. 28, Autumn, p. 14.

Open University (1981) *Curriculum in Action: An Approach to Evaluation*, Open University Press, Milton Keynes.

Osborn, A. F. and Milbank, J. E. (1987) *The Effects of Early Education*, Clarendon Press, Oxford.

Pen Green Family Centre (1990) *Learning to be Strong*, Changing Perspectives, Northwich.

Pugh, G. (1988) *Services for Under Fives. Developing a Co-ordinated Approach*, National Children's Bureau, London.

Pugh, G. and De'Ath, E. (1989) *Working Towards Partnership in the Early Years*, National Children's Bureau, London.

Renvoize, J. (1974) *Children in Danger*, Routledge & Kegan Paul, London.

Richards, R. (1987) Learning through Science in the Early Years, in G. A. Blenkin and A. V. Kelly (eds.) op. cit., pp. 218–30.

Riley, D. (1983) *War in the Nursery*, Virago, London.

Schools Council (1984) *Guidelines for Internal Review and Development in Schools*, Longman, London.

Schweinhart, L. J., Weikart, D. P. and Larner, M.B. (1986) Consequences of Three Preschool Curriculum Models through Age 15, *Early Childhood Quarterly*, Vol. 1, no. 1, pp. 15-45.

Smith, P. K. (ed.) (1984) *Play in Animals and Humans*, Blackwell, Oxford.

Smith, T. (1980) *Parents and Preschool*, Grant McIntyre, London.

Stevenson, C. (1987) The Young Four Year Old in Nursery and Infant Classes: Challenges and Constraints, in NFER/SCDC, op. cit., pp. 34–43.

Stubbs, D. R. (1985) *Assertiveness at Work*, Gower Publishing, London.

Thomas, G. (1988) 'Hallo, Miss Scatterbrain. Hallo, Mr Strong': Assessing Attitudes and Behaviour in the Nursery, in A. Cohen and L. Cohen (eds.) *Early Education: The Pre-School Years*, Paul Chapman, London, p. 227–41.

Tizard, B., Mortimore, J. and Burchell, B. (1981) *Involving Parents in Nursery and Infant Schools*, Grant McIntyre, London.

Tizard, B. and Hughes, M. (1984) *Young Children Learning*, Fontana, London.

Tizard, B., Blatchford, P., Burke, J., Farquhar, C. and Plewis, I. (1988) *Young Children at School in the Inner City*, Lawrence Erlbaum Associates, Hove.

Tyler, S. (1979) *Keele Preschool Assessment Guide*, NFER/Nelson, Windsor.

Watt, J. (1977) *Co-operation in Preschool Education*, SSRC, London.

Wells, G. (1986) *The Meaning Makers. Children Learning Language and Using Language to Learn*, Hodder & Stoughton, Sevenoaks.

Whitehead, M. (1990) *Language and Literacy in the Early Years. An Approach for Education Students*, Paul Chapman, London.

Whyte, J. (1983) *Beyond the Wendy House: Sex Role Stereotyping in Primary Schools*, Longman for Schools Council, York.

Wicks, M. (1989) Family Trends, Insecurities and Social Policy, in *Children and Society*, Vol. 3, no. 1, pp. 67-80, National Children's Bureau, London.

Wolfendale, S. (1987) *All About Me*, National Children's Bureau, London.

Wood, D., McMahon, L. and Cranstoun, Y. (1980) *Working with Under Fives*, Grant McIntyre, London.

ORGANIZATIONS REFERRED TO IN THE TEXT

BAECE (British Association for Early Childhood Education) details from: 111 City View, 463 Bethnal Green Road, London E2 9QH.

EYCG (Early Years Curriculum Group) details from: Vicky Hurst, Faculty of Education, Goldsmiths' College, Lewisham Way, London SE14 6NW.

NCNE (National Campaign for Nursery Education) details from: 23 Albert Street, London NW1 7LU.

TACTYC (Tutors of Advanced Courses for Teachers of Young Children) details from: BCM Box 5342, London WC1N 3XX.

AUTHOR INDEX

SUBJECT INDEX